Great Medical Discoveries

Tuberculosis

by Gail B. Stewart

Other books in the Great Medical Discoveries series:

Cloning
Gene Therapy
Vaccines

Library of Congress Cataloging-in-Publication Data

EG
Stewart, Gail B., 1949–
  Tuberculosis / by Gail B. Stewart.
    p. cm. — (Great medical discoveries)
Includes bibliographical references and index.
Summary: Looks at the history, diagnosis, treatment, and
ongoing threat of tuberculosis, which continues to be the
most deadly infectious disease in the world.
  ISBN 1-56006-931-7
  1. Tuberculosis—Juvenile literature. [1. Tuberculosis. 2.
Diseases.] I. Title. II. Series.
  RC311.1 .S72 2002

2001004871

Copyright © 2002 by Lucent Books, Inc.
Lucent Books 10911 Technology Place, San Diego, CA 92127
Printed in the U.S.A.

CONTENTS

FOREWORD

Throughout history, people have struggled to understand and conquer the diseases and physical ailments that plague us. Once in a while, a discovery has changed the course of medicine and sometimes, the course of history itself. The stories of these discoveries have many elements in common—accidental findings, sudden insights, human dedication, and most of all, powerful results. Many illnesses that in the past were essentially a death warrant for their sufferers are today curable or even virtually extinct. And exciting new directions in medicine promise a future in which the building blocks of human life itself—the genes—may be manipulated and altered to restore health or to prevent disease from occurring in the first place.

It has been said that an insight is simply a rearrangement of already-known facts, and as often as not, these great medical discoveries have resulted partly from a reexamination of earlier efforts in light of new knowledge. Nineteenth-century monk Gregor Mendel experimented with pea plants for years, quietly unlocking the mysteries of genetics. However, the importance of his findings went unnoticed until three separate scientists, studying cell division with a newly improved invention called a microscope, rediscovered his work decades after his death. French doctor Jean-Antoine Villemin's experiments with rabbits proved that tuberculosis was contagious, but his conclusions were politely ignored by the medical community until another doctor, Robert Koch of Germany, discovered the exact culprit—the tubercle bacillus germ—years later.

Accident, too, has played a part in some medical discoveries. Because the tuberculosis germ does not stain with dye as easily as other bacteria, Koch was able to see it only after he had let a treated slide sit far longer than he intended. An unwanted speck of mold led Englishman Alexander Fleming to recognize the bacteria-killing qualities of the penicillium fungi, ushering in the era of antibiotic "miracle drugs."

That researchers sometimes benefited from fortu- itous accidents does not mean that they were bum- bling amateurs who relied solely on luck. They were dedicated scientists whose work created the condi- tions under which such lucky events could occur; many sacrificed years of their lives to observation and experimentation. Sometimes the price they paid was higher. René Laënnec, who invented the stetho- scope to help him study the effects of tuberculosis, himself succumbed to the disease.

And humanity has benefited from these scientists' efforts. The formerly terrifying disease of smallpox has been eliminated from the face of the earth—the only case of the complete conquest of a once deadly disease. Tuberculosis, perhaps the oldest disease known to humans and certainly one of its most prolific killers, has been essentially wiped out in some parts of the world. Genetically engineered insulin is a godsend to countless diabetics who are allergic to the animal insulin that has traditionally been used to help them.

Despite such triumphs there are few unequivocal success stories in the history of great medical discov- eries. New strains of tuberculosis are proving to be resistant to the antibiotics originally developed to treat them, raising the specter of a resurgence of the disease that has killed 2 billion people over the course of human history. But medical research continues on numerous fronts and will no doubt lead to still undreamed-of advancements in the future.

Each volume in the Great Medical Discoveries series tells the story of one great medical breakthrough—the first gropings for understanding, the pieces that came together and how, and the immediate and longer-term results. Part science and part social history, the series explains some of the key findings that have shaped modern medicine and relieved untold human suffering. Numerous primary and secondary source quotations enhance the text and bring to life all the drama of scientific discovery. Sidebars highlight personalities and convey personal stories. The series also discusses the future of each medical discovery—a future in which vaccines may guard against AIDS, gene therapy may eliminate cancer, and other as-yet unimagined treatments may become commonplace.

INTRODUCTION

The Disease That Survived Its Own Death

The disease had killed more people than any in the history of the world—more than the plague known as the Black Death, more than influenza, more than cholera. In two centuries, it had ended the lives of 1 billion people around the world. It was no wonder, then, that in the late 1940s when rumors circulated about new drugs being developed that seemed to be promising cures for tuberculosis, people were excited.

A patient rests in a sanatorium, a special medical facility in which tuberculosis patients relax and recover.

The excitement grew as tests showed the drugs worked on tuberculosis germs, first in mice, then in a monkey. After determining that the drugs would be safe to try on humans, researchers allowed doctors at Sea View Hospital in New York to begin injecting the drugs into patients who were dying of tuberculosis. Most of these patients were skeletally thin and had no appetite. Many had high fevers. All had severe coughs that produced a lot of sputum, or phlegm, loaded with tuberculosis germs.

Dancing in the Wards

The results were beyond anything doctors had predicted. Not only did symptoms ease, many disappeared within twenty-four hours. Feverish temperatures dropped to normal; patients who had picked at their food earlier now ate ravenously. "They called for third and fourth helpings of cereal," one reporter wrote, "and many worked up from one egg at breakfast to five. One old man got his ration up to eleven."[1]

Every one of the patients who had been given the drugs gained weight. The weight gain gave a great boost of energy to people who had been too sick to even sit up without help. Many who had been bedridden for months were walking around the wards within a few days of receiving the injection.

Word of the apparent cure spread rapidly. Newspaper reporters from all over the United States visited the hospital and gave the "wonder drugs" front-page status. Noted a *Time* magazine article, "Patients who had taken the drugs danced in the wards, to the delight of news photographers."[2] A widely circulated news photo showed a dozen laughing, dancing women and bore the caption: "A few months ago, only the sound of TB victims coughing their lives away could be heard here."[3]

It seemed then that science had triumphed. The disease that had decimated populations all over the world would no longer be a threat, although, it might take some time for less developed countries to achieve such results, and cases of the disease might still crop up from time to time. Even so, predicted one expert, "[Tuberculosis] is expected to cease to be a public health problem, and before the end of this century it may become so rare in the United States as to constitute a medical curiosity."[4] The predictions appeared to have come true; by the 1980s, TB had all but disappeared. Like polio, cholera, and smallpox, tuberculosis could be added to the list of casualties in the war with modern science.

An Unbelievable Diagnosis

Yet just over forty years after the apparent conquest of tuberculosis, in the town of La Quinta, California, the parents of one teenage girl were frantic. They had watched their healthy daughter change drastically in a short time. Once active and involved in her high school, in 1993 Debi French had become tired and listless. She had a cough she had not been able to shake. She had no energy. She was losing weight, too.

Doctors thought at first it might be a virus—perhaps a persistent flu bug. However, as the weeks went by and Debi worsened, such an explanation seemed less likely. To determine the cause of her racking cough, her doctors ordered a chest X ray. What they discovered astonished them all.

The diagnosis was tuberculosis—and a very aggressive case, too. Only by flying Debi to a special treatment center in Colorado and removing part of her lung were doctors able to save her life. Far from living in poverty in a developing nation, Debi was part of an upper-middle-class community. Nor was Debi the only one who was infected; soon afterward, 178 students and staff at her high school tested positive for tuberculosis.

What Is Happening?

The outbreak of tuberculosis in California more than forty years after the disease was supposed to have been conquered seems impossible. Even more incredible are the statistics about this disease that was predicted in 1953 to become a "medical curiosity" by now.

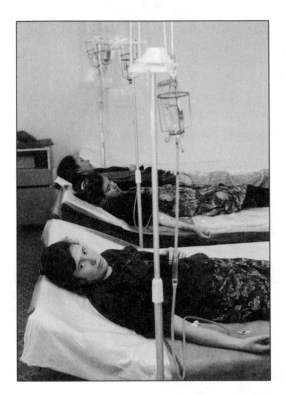

Tuberculosis patients receive medicine and nourishment intravenously.

Tuberculosis is still the single leading cause of death from an infectious disease in the world today. According to medical authorities, 8 million new cases of it are diagnosed each year, and 2 million people die of it. Once believed to be on the brink of extinction, tuberculosis has made a comeback, much to the dismay of the medical community. Admits one researcher, "We declared victory too soon."[5]

Tuberculosis threatens to become even more widespread—and at the same time, more deadly—in the years to come. Researchers say that in some communities, the rate of infection is more than 30 percent. These same researchers know, too, that because of the ease with which people travel from continent to continent today, no matter where the disease crops up, it has the potential to affect anyone, anywhere. Says Lee Reichman of the National Tuberculosis Center in New Jersey, "TB anywhere is a threat here."[6]

It is remarkable that the status of tuberculosis changed so drastically within such a short time. Tuberculosis went from being one of humankind's most deadly diseases, to being considered a thing of the past in the mid-twentieth century. How it seemed to be vanquished, and then was able to reemerge in a more deadly form than ever, is a story that is both frustrating and frightening.

CHAPTER 1

The White Plague

Tuberculosis, often shortened to TB, has existed since before the beginning of written history. In fact, scientists say that tuberculosis—called by a variety of names over the centuries—may be one of the oldest diseases on earth.

Seven Millennia of Tuberculosis

The disease known as tuberculosis can take various forms. The most serious form affects the pulmonary system—especially the lungs. But the tuberculosis germ can also destroy skin cells, lymph nodes, and brain tissue.

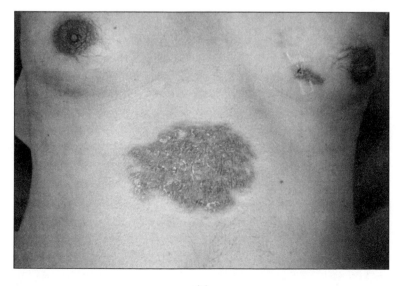

Some forms of TB can cause lesions to form on the skin.

Tuberculosis germs are capable of gouging holes in bones, too—especially those of the spine. This form of TB is known today as Pott's disease. As vertebrae are destroyed, the upper spine may collapse, giving the sufferer of this disease a hunchbacked look. The long bones of the legs and arms can sometimes be affected as well.

Using these facts, scientists have found evidence of tuberculosis in a skeleton found in southern Europe that dates back to 5000 B.C. Evidence in another ancient grave found in Italy shows that tuberculosis caused the death of a fifteen-year-old boy during the Stone Age—approximately 4000 B.C.

Egyptian tombs show that tuberculosis was common during the times of the pharaohs. The remains of kings such as Tutankhamen, who died in 1352 B.C., show evidence of the disease, and murals decorating the tombs show many figures with the telltale hunchback.

The disease plagued not only Africa and Europe but also prehistoric North America. (Tuberculosis was one of the few epidemics that was not inadvertently brought from Europe to afflict native peoples in North and South America.) The gouged-out vertebrae evident in Indian burial sites proves that tuberculosis existed among ancient Huron Indian people, as well as among native peoples in Peru and Mexico.

A Variety of Names

Tuberculosis is its modern name, but the pulmonary form of the disease was known as *phthisis* (meaning "to waste away") among the ancient Greeks. They considered it the most dangerous of all diseases, noting that it seemed to be especially prevalent among young people. Indeed, as one historian notes, "Pale, emaciated youths, fighting for breath, coughing up blood and dying young were as common in the Antique world as were the wonderfully fit horsemen who paraded on the frieze of the Parthenon."[7]

The ancient Greeks gave one of the most complete early descriptions of the physical symptoms of the disease in its later stages. The physician Aretaeus, who lived in the second century A.D., observed the following in one of his patients:

> Voice hoarse; neck slightly bent, tender and stiff; fingers slender but the joints swollen; severe wasting of the fleshy parts leaving the bones prominently outlined; the nails crooked or flat and brittle without their normal rotundity. . . . The nose is sharp and slender, the cheeks are prominently and abnormally flushed; the eyes are deeply sunk in their hollows but brilliant and glittering. . . . The slender parts of the jaws rest on the teeth as if smiling but it is the smile of cadavers. . . . The shoulder blades are like the wings of birds.[8]

Swine Dung and Buttered Feet

Some of the ancient physicians had ideas on the best way to accurately diagnose the disease, as well as cure it. Galen, a contemporary of Aretaeus, was convinced that blood in the sputum was a sure way to diagnose the disease. If the patient's condition had deteriorated to the point where he or she was clammy and feverish, Galen believed there was little hope for recovery.

However, Galen suggested that if the patient was not yet feverish, the feet should be soaked in a potion of lupine leaves (related to the pea plant) and myrrh oil. After a certain length of time, the potion should be rinsed from the skin, and the patient's feet should then be smeared with butter.

About the same time, the Roman physician Pliny suggested health-restoring foods as cures for tuberculosis. For a seriously ill patient, he prescribed either the flesh of a female donkey made into a broth or the ashes of swine dung mixed into raisin wine.

The King's Evil

None of these early remedies helped much, and the death rates from this curious disease

Galen, an ancient Greek physician.

The Possible Cure by Horseback Riding

Beginning as far back as the eighth century, some doctors have advised their patients of the value of horseback riding, not only as a means of preventing illness, but specifically as a cure for tuberculosis, then called "phthisis." In The White Plague: Tuberculosis, Man, and Society, *René and Jean Dubos cite an explanation from eighteenth-century English philosopher John Locke on the merits of riding.*

Ye Doctor sent him into ye Count on Horseback (tho he was soe weak yt he could hardly walk), & ordered him to ride six or seven miles ye first day (which he did) & to encrease dayly his journey as he shd be able, until he had rid one hundred and fifty miles: When he had travelld half ye way his Diarrhoea stopt, & at last he came to ye end of his journey & was pretty well (at least somewhat better) & he had a good appetite; but when he had staid at his Sister's house some four or five days his Diarrhoea came on again; the Doctor had ordered him not to stay above two days at most; for if they stay before they are recovered this spoils all again; & therefore he betook himself to his riding again, and in four days he came up to London perfectly cured. The same course hath ye Doctor put others upon, especially in Pulmonick Diseases, & with ye like success when all things else had failed him; and he was not ashamed to own ty he was fain to borrow a cure from this way and now and then when he found himself pyzzled with some lingering distemper nor reducible to a common and known disease.

in its various forms continued. The form of TB that affected the lymph glands was known by the Latin word *scrofula*, meaning "little pig." The reference has two possible explanations. The first was that pigs often suffered from diseases that made their necks lumpy and swollen, like those of the people suffering from this sort of TB. The other widely held possibility was that the necks of people who suffered from scrofula became so swollen and distended that the people were thought to resemble little pigs.

Scrofula was also referred to as "the king's evil" in parts of Europe because the belief was that certain kings had received healing powers from God, and scrofula was one of the diseases that was most susceptible to a king's powerful blessing. Some people were said to have been cured within hours of receiving a royal touch. In the late eleventh century, during the reign of England's Edward the Confessor, a ritual was introduced into the Church, at which people suffering from scrofula would be presented to the king. King Edward I would dip his fingers in water and touch each person as he or she passed by.

Yet while some were reported cured, the need for the ritual continued over the centuries. There was no shortage of customers either, and the blessings were performed twice each month, with an extra session on Christmas Eve and on Easter Sunday. In one month during the thirteenth century, King Edward I touched 533 scrofula sufferers. Philip Augustus of France touched 1,500 sufferers in one six-hour ceremony—a feat outdone centuries later by Louis XIV, who touched 1,600 in an Easter Sunday ritual.

Interestingly, the ritual continued to be performed even after the idea of kings having God-given healing powers was no longer in fashion. The last monarch to perform the ceremony was Queen Anne, only a little girl when she came to the British throne. So desperate were the scrofula sufferers for her final touching ritual in 1714 that several were trampled to death in the line at the back of the church. Unfortunately, although the ritual was discontinued early in the eighteenth century, the disease was more common than ever before.

By the end of the seventeenth century, tuberculosis was responsible for 20 percent of the deaths in Wales and England, with the greatest rate of new cases found in the cities. Hospitals were established in various European cities to care for those who had not been helped by the royal touch ceremonies—and historians say that these facilities were filled to capacity. The hospitals could make the sick more comfortable, although they had little to offer in the way of a cure.

Sylvius's Observations

Many European doctors were beginning to call the pulmonary form of the disease—by far the most deadly—"consumption," for it appeared to consume, or eat away at, the strength and energy of those who were suffering from it. But because of the increasing numbers of people who were dying from it—about 7 million each year—and because in many cases the sufferers acquired a pale complexion, the disease was also becoming known as "the white plague."

This plague had no cure and no promising leads that pointed to the possibility of a cure. However, by the end of the seventeenth century, changes were taking place in the way medicine was being taught. Scientists were starting to look for causes of disease rather than being satisfied with noting symptoms. To accomplish this goal, medical schools began to dissect the bodies of dead patients, hoping to find answers.

One of the leading anatomy teachers of the day was a Prussian named Sylvius, who in 1679 noticed the presence of little, hard nodules in the lungs of people who had died of consumption. Since they were not present in those who had died of other ailments, they seemed to be definitely related to the disease. Sylvius called these nodules "tubercles," from the Latin word *tuberulum*, meaning "little swelling."

Tubercles appeared in different forms. Some were smooth and hard, grayish-pink in color. Others were whitish and had a cheesy consistency. The larger tubercles were often filled with pus—though what that meant, or where the tubercles came from, no one knew.

Thomas Young studied TB in the early nineteenth century.

Questions and Fears

Sylvius's discovery was interesting but seemed to lead nowhere. Understandably, doctors were frustrated. How did a person become ill with the disease? Was it spread somehow from person to person, or was it inherited? What role did the tubercles play? All that could be said for certain as the years went by was that no other disease posed more of a threat than this one. Early in the nineteenth century, a French doctor noted, "There is no more dangerous disease . . . and no other is so common. . . . [I]t destroys a very great part of the human race."[9]

In 1815, Thomas Young published a *Historical and Practical Treatise on Consumptive*

Diseases. Young described consumption as "a disease so frequent as to carry off prematurely about one-fourth part of the inhabitants of Europe, and so fatal as often to deter the practitioner even from attempting a cure."[10]

In the United States at this same time, the number of consumptive patients was ballooning—and people were beginning to panic. Indeed, it was difficult to find a family in the early nineteenth century that had not lost at least one member to the disease. Dr. Joseph Gallup reported in 1816 that in six years he had three times as many consumptive patients as he had had in the sixteen years before that. One prominent Massachusetts woman who had seen several neighbors die of consumption admitted her fear of the disease, "which may be marching forth [through] this land to seize me with that firm grasp which will surely . . . lead me to the grave."[11]

Author Robert Louis Stevenson was one of the more famous people to have tuberculosis.

A Fashionable Disease

The age group hardest hit by consumption seemed to be teenagers and young adults. Accounts abound of young people wasting away before they had experienced life. In addition, a large number of prominent young artists, writers, and musicians fell victim to the disease in the 1800s. Perhaps this is the reason why, although a diagnosis of consumption was virtually a death sentence, it was also fashionable.

Having consumption put a person in a class with people such as poet John Keats, authors Robert Louis Stevenson and the Brontë sisters, and composer Frédéric Chopin—a few of the famous people who had fallen to the disease. To suffer in the same way was almost a badge of distinction. During the early part of the nineteenth century, writes historian Mark Caldwell, "of all diseases, [consumption] had a reputation more calculated to draw admiration than repulsion."[12]

Part of the reason for this admiration was that consumption was a slower, gentler killer than other epidemics that sprang up from time to time. Cholera, for example, would exhibit itself with violent cramping, diarrhea, and vomiting. Death usually followed after just a few days of excruciatingly painful symptoms. Malaria, which usually killed people within one to three weeks, was marked by high fever, chills, headache, and vomiting.

But consumption was by definition a wasting away— a slow process that could take as long as five years to snuff out the life of a sufferer. The symptoms were less severe, too: a cough, lack of energy, pale skin, and weight loss. Many people of the mid-1800s (often called the Victorian era) found these symptoms neither particularly unpleasant nor frightening to be around. After all, during this time period, a robust, tan body—especially in a woman—was considered vulgar.

"A Painless, Poetical Death"

The very white skin tone, the eyes sparkling with fever, and the emaciated body of a consumptive person actually appealed to many American and British young people, says one historian, as consumption "set the standard for white middle-class beauty in the mid-nineteenth century."[13] The look was alluring to people such as writer Edgar Allan Poe, who would later die of consumption himself. His first wife, Virginia, had the disease; he wrote of the lovely picture she made one evening during a party at their home. Dressed in white, Virginia was "delicately, morbidly angelic," and while playing the harp, she suddenly "stopped, clutched her throat and a wave of crimson blood ran down her breast. . . . It rendered her even more ethereal."[14]

Because so many artists in various fields suffered from consumption, the image of the consumptive hero or heroine was reflected in literature and art of the time. Operas such as *La Traviata* by Verdi and *La Bohème* by Puccini relied on characters dying of consumption, as did novels such as Charles Dickens's *David Copperfield* and Emily Brontë's *Wuthering Heights*.

According to René and Jean Dubos, writing in *The White Plague*, an incurable cold that settled in a character's lungs was a frequent device in a great number of Victorian novels. They explain: "Consumption served the purpose well, since it was believed to affect chiefly sensitive natures, and conferred upon them a refined physical charm before making them succumb to a painless, poetical death." [15]

The Look Without the Disease

The fascination with the consumptive look was so strong that even those who were healthy wanted to look like they were ill. The poet Lord Byron said to a friend in 1828, "I look pale. I should like to die of consumption." When asked why, he replied, "The ladies would all say, 'Look at that poor Byron, how interesting he looks in dying!'" [16]

Fashions and trends of the day reflected Byron's view. It became fashionable for women to use whitening powder instead of rouge. Some even added a touch of blue to the powder to give their skin an almost transparent look. Carrying a large handkerchief and coughing delicately into it helped complete the image.

Wearing clothes with very high collars was a style rooted in consumption, too. For instance, many who suffered from scrofula were self-conscious about the swollen glands in their necks and often used frilly, high collars to hide them. The look gained popularity as many healthy men and women adopted the style to look as though they, too, suffered from scrofula.

Women became more anxious than ever before to lose large amounts of weight. "Because young men of fashion had developed . . . a passion for pale young women apparently dying of consumption," writes

The appearance of having TB became very fashionable, and women began wearing dresses like this one that emphasized a thin waist.

one researcher, "young women took to drinking lemon juice and vinegar to kill their appetites and make themselves look more alluring."[17] Nor was it only women who felt the need to appear skeleton thin. One French poet insisted that he would not have been taken seriously at the time unless he became gaunt. "I could not have been accepted as a poet," he said, "weighing more than 99 pounds."[18]

A Second Look

The view that consumption was a disease of the creative soul was a distorted one. However, the publicity given to those celebrities who had the disease seemed to lend support to the view. Besides, doctors were completely unclear about what the source of the disease was. For a short time, the idea that it was an expression of an artistic character did not seem far-fetched at all.

But by the 1870s, even though medical experts still were puzzled about how the disease spread, consumption was clearly becoming a disease of the poor. As the industrial revolution progressed and more and more factory workers were crowding into the cities, the consumption rate skyrocketed.

As one historian explains, the same writers who just a few years before were describing the disease as having roots in the arts, had to acknowledge a much different idea:

> They saw hosts of men, women, and children, pale too, often cold and starving, working long hours in dark and crowded shops, breathing smoke and coal dust. Tuberculosis was there, breeding suffering and misery without romance. . . .
>
> In the laboring classes consumption was not the aristocratic decline, inspiring works of art. . . . It was the great killer and breeder of destitution.[19]

A New Search for Causes

As consumption became known as a disease of the masses, medical experts of the time were forced to explore new ideas about what caused it. The most popular theory in the late nineteenth century was that certain people had a susceptibility to consumption—usually because of inborn, or inherited, weaknesses.

The idea of heredity made sense because the disease often seemed to run in families. Some examples were well known, such as the Brontë family, in which all six children, as well as their father, died of consumption. Far more examples were found among ordinary people, such as a family in France in which all five children were healthy until they reached age thirty, when they promptly died of consumption—one after another.

Doctors were not sure that the disease itself was hereditary; they believed it was far more likely that a physical flaw passed down from parents to children, made people susceptible to developing the disease. It was the second part of the cause—one's environment—that provided the opportunity for consumption to enter a healthy body and kill it.

Spotting the Flawed

Some scientists believed that a smart doctor could tell just by looking at patients if they had some hereditary weakness that might make them more susceptible to consumption. Sir James Clarke, whose 1835 textbook on consumption was considered a physician's best resource at the time, gave a detailed portrait of how such a weakness would appear:

> Tradition and common observation clearly show why some individuals rather than others become consumptive. These unfortunates are instantly recognizable by their scrawny body, flat, narrow or concave chest, fair freckled skin, red or very pale hair and eyes, [and] irregularly harsh instead of silky breathing."[20]

Other doctors identified personality traits that they believed weakened a person's ability to resist consumption. Some cited weaknesses such as the inability to organize one's studies, too much concern over seeking pleasure, the overuse of alcohol, and, with women in particular, the wearing of immoderate clothing. Historians today point out that many of the so-called flaws were often based on biased, stereotyped views that upper-class doctors of the time commonly held.

For instance, many doctors claimed that the city-dwelling poor were more susceptible because they were more likely to be careless about their hygiene and to feel depressing emotions—two more signs of weakness. Another widely held belief was that certain ethnic or racial groups were more susceptible than others because of their supposed inherent weaknesses. The Irish were prone to negative thoughts and the abuse of alcohol, according to medical claims of the time. Africans, too, were believed to be far more likely to become consumptive. Said one doctor, "The [African's] small lung capacity as compared with that of the white, and his deficient brain capacity render him less resistant to the disease when once acquired."[21]

Doctors believed that the city-dwelling poor, like this family, were more susceptible to tuberculosis because of careless hygiene.

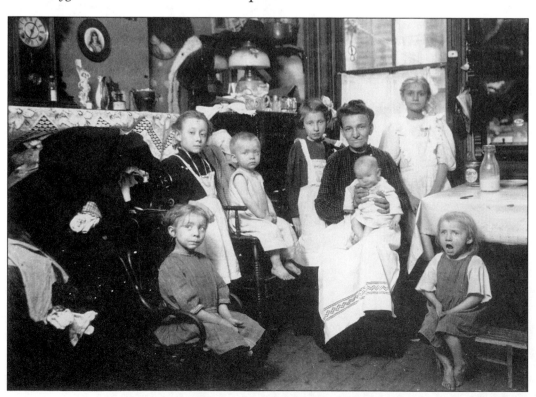

Frightening Array of New Cures

As these questionable new theories about the causes of consumption arose, so too did a host of new remedies that were equally ill conceived. Some of these supposed cures were simply useless, while others were downright dangerous.

A traveling salesman sells a home remedy. People believed these remedies could cure TB as well as several other illnesses.

As in the past, traveling salesmen sold a great many potions, ointments, and pills that were touted as "miracle drugs." Iodine was one of these new medicines, and some doctors urged their patients to drink it, rub it on their chests, or add it to bathwater. Besides being expensive, iodine was criticized as causing severe problems with the nervous system, while doing nothing for consumption.

One supposed cure that was far more harmful was called "cupping." Cupping was related to a much older practice of bleeding a sick person to rid the body of impurities. While bleeding had all but disappeared by the end of the nineteenth century, cupping had not. The object was to draw out the source of consumption by making an incision with a scalpel and applying a preheated glass cup with rough edges. "As the cup and the air within it cooled and contracted," explains one researcher, "blood and tissue and sometimes pus and other . . . material oozed out through the incision."[22] Patients subjected to cupping frequently went into shock, because of the large amount of blood lost in so short a time. Those who avoided shock often died after their wounds from the process became seriously infected.

Many cultures believed that blood was crucial to the healing of consumption. Consumptive patients were frequently urged to drink the blood of a healthy animal.

A Selection of Strange Cures

In his book, The White Death: A History of Tuberculosis, *Thomas Dormandy cites some of the strangest cure ideas for advanced tuberculosis proposed during the eighteenth and early nineteenth centuries.*

For "patients who looked healthy enough," Dr. John Travers of the Brompton Hospital recommended two grains of antimony tartrate dissolved in gentian water and "as soon as nausea commences a nutmeg size electuary of quinine, sulphurous sublimate, potassium nitrate, and antimony sulphate kneaded together with gum." Hydrocyanic acid was deemed "most useful for asthenic [slender] patients." Dr. Samuel Fillimore of Glasgow found creosote in various forms "a most serviceable standby." None of these preparations were ever subjected to anything resembling a controlled trial: when in the 1880s Austin Flint of New York first suggested that some "of our cherished remedies" should be subjected to such an investigation, his proposal caused great hilarity among the grandees [prestigious doctors] of Harley Street [a fashionable district of London]. . . .

Country folk, too, though they could not afford such complicated remedies, believed in the inhalation of the exhaled warm breath of healthy beasts. In Suffolk, the source had to be a stallion, in Herefordshire a piebald horse, in the Scottish Lowlands a cow and in the Highlands a sheep. . . . [The author] Balzac described a Swiss peasant who cured himself of consumption by breathing in the thick air of his cowhouse. The effluvium of maggoty meat was a popular folk remedy in many parts of France, Austria, Hungary, and Poland well into the twentieth century.

One visitor to Denver, Colorado, described a group of consumptive patients involved in what was called the "slaughterhouse cure":

> Every day the death of oxen and cows was anticipated as a renewed life to men and women. When the doors of the slaughterhouse opened, a throng rushed in ready to catch the ebbing life of the doomed animals. As the warm red current gushed forth, glasses were held to be filled from the stream [of blood].[23]

Among the most ghoulish consequences of this practice, however, was the belief of some physicians that human blood was even more effective against consumption than animal blood. People were even killed for their blood. In one instance, an eight-year-old boy was kidnapped and brought to the house of a wealthy man dying of the disease. The man's physician believed that human blood was the man's last chance at survival. "Unmoved by the boy's cries and prayers," reported one source at the time, "the attendant quack plunged a knife into his left axilla [armpit] and the patient drank the blood while the boy was dying."[24]

Lard, Gas, and Boa Constrictors

Some of the other new cures were less gruesome but still baseless. English doctor Edgar Spilsbury found that butchers rarely seemed to be consumptive. He wondered if perhaps their immunity was due to the fat that they always had on their hands. Spilsbury claimed that he had cured at least four patients by rubbing beef lard onto their bodies.

Another doctor reported instant relief of chest pain and cough by taking a preparation of excreta (solid waste) from a boa constrictor, mixed with water.

A particularly painful treatment involved pumping various gas mixtures into the bodies of patients. "Patients lay immersed in gas-filled rooms for hours," reports one historian, "or used complicated . . . inhalers resembling steam engines." Not convinced that the gas reached the lungs if pumped orally, one doctor pumped

Isolating the TB Patient

In his 1906 book, Consumption: Its Relation to Man and His Civilization, Its Prevention and Cure, *author John Bessner Huber discusses the sixteenth-century notion of isolating the tuberculosis patient and taking care to vigorously clean a room after he or she has died. Even though the details of germ theory were not understood completely, many of these precautions are still followed today.*

The present day tendency with regard to the separation of phthisical patients in hospitals had its forerunner in 1760, when a hospital was erected in Olivuzza for the special accommodation of phthisical patients, who were moved there out of other hospitals in order that they not spread the infection. The modern sanatorium is based upon much the same idea.

In 1782 an edict was issued at Naples ordering the isolation of consumptives and the disinfection of their furniture, books, etc. Except for its historic atmosphere, this decree is in substance much like a circular issued by a modern health board.

Thus: "The Deputies in this capital and the Governors of Locum Tenens in the Provinces should, immediately after the burial of a phthisical patient, be sure to have his rooms cleansed, the floors, wainscoting and ceiling renewed, the wooden doors and windows scrubbed and cleansed, and fresh plants introduced in order that the corrupt and infectious atmosphere may not be communicated to persons who live near; also that they should make use of any other precautions which physicians use in like cases." . . .

The following penalties were imposed in this decree:

"Those who oppose the officials making their inventories, isolating or removing the clothes to the crematorium, and the cleansing of the places where the patient died, shall be sentenced to three years at the galleys or prison according to the condition of the person, and shall have three years imprisonment and three hundred ducats fine."

it into his patients' rectum, "whence [it was] sure to reach the lungs."[25]

Not surprisingly, the outlook for a cure for the most prolific killer in the world was bleak in the latter half of the nineteenth century. Almost nothing was understood about consumption, except that nothing doctors tried appeared to slow or halt its progress. But great discoveries on the horizon would allow researchers a more accurate picture of the disease that was killing more people than ever before.

CHAPTER 2

Fighting Tuberculosis

S ome of the advances in the fight against tuberculosis were dramatic—an experiment or discovery that was wildly successful, such as the advent in the early 1950s of the first antibiotics effective against TB. More common, however, were the quieter successes. These were frequently new combinations of ideas or discoveries that had been around for years—sometimes even centuries. But for whatever reason, the medical community did not understand or appreciate them when they were initially introduced. Only after a second or third look at these discoveries did their value become recognized.

One such advance was the stethoscope, a device that was invented in 1816. While it could neither cure nor prevent consumption, it proved extremely useful in accurately diagnosing and understanding more about the disease decades later.

Hearing Tuberculosis

The idea that it was helpful for a physician to hear the sounds within the human body—breathing, heartbeat, and so on—was not new when the French doctor René Laënnec devised the stethoscope. A few of the ancient Greeks had noted certain sounds in the chest in patients who were close to death. And in the early 1700s, the scientist Robert Hooke had written about how common it

27

was "to hear the motion of the wind to and fro in the guts and other small vessels," and had predicted that someday "it may be possible to discover the motions of the internal parts of bodies . . . by the sounds they make."[26]

One hundred years after Hooke's prophecy, doctors were occasionally putting an ear to the chest of a patient, but there were limitations. With certain patients it was difficult to hear distinct sounds—in women because of the layer of breast tissue, and in very overweight patients because of layers of fat.

Laënnec, a young doctor interested in consumption and other lung diseases, solved the problem. He wrote later that he had remembered an interesting bit of trivia he had learned as a boy, "namely, if one places one ear at the end of a piece of timber one can hear very distinctly the scratch of a pin at the other end."[27]

Applying the same principle, Laënnec rolled up a piece of stiff notebook paper into a tight tube and, placing one end on a consumptive patient's chest and the other to his own ear, was able to hear chest sounds clearly. Pleased with the device, he made some hollow wooden tubes, experimenting with shape and size.

More than a Toy

He called the device a "stethoscope" from the Greek words *stethus*, meaning "chest," and *skop*, meaning "to see." Some of his fellow physicians sniffed at the idea of the stethoscope, but most found it interesting.

Admittedly, for many doctors Laënnec's stethoscope was little more than a novelty. Most did not have the ability to discern any differences between the types of lung sounds they heard in their patients. However, Laënnec was knowledgeable about consumption. He had taken part in the autopsies of patients with consumption and had noted the various stages of tubercles that Sylvius had first described in the seventeenth century.

Combining that knowledge with what he could learn from living patients using his stethoscope, Laënnec was able to do an amazing amount of research on consumption. Interested in the differences in sound between consumption and other lung diseases, he learned to sharpen his listening. Eventually, Laënnec's trained ear could differentiate the various sounds—wheeze, rattle, gurgle, whistle, and so on—and could often tell if a patient was suffering from consumption or from another disease, such as bronchitis or pneumonia. Furthermore, if the diagnosis was consumption, Laënnec was usually able to pinpoint how advanced the disease was and whether the tubercles were large or small, hard or of a cheesy consistency. Eventually he was able to accurately predict what an autopsy of a dead patient's lungs would show.

Laënnec believed that the tubercle at its tiniest size was the first stage of consumption. He wanted to learn exactly how the varied sizes and consistencies of the tubercles affected the lungs, but he was not able to finish

Mocking Laënnec

Not everyone was convinced of the value of René Laënnec's stethoscope when he first introduced it. Some thought it a trifle—no more important than a toy or a magic trick. One of Laënnec's harshest critics was John Forbes; his rather scornful assessment of the stethoscope is excerpted from René and Jean Dubos's

The White Plague: Tuberculosis, Man, and Society.

That it will ever come into general use notwithstanding its value, I am extremely doubtful; because its beneficial application requires much time and gives a good deal of trouble both to the patient and the practitioner; because its whole hue and character are foreign, and opposed to all our habits and associations. It must be confessed that there is something even ludicrous in the picture of a grave physician proudly listening through a long tube applied to the patient's thorax, as if the disease were a living being that could communicate its condition to the sense without. Besides, there is in this method a sort of bold claim and pretension to certainty and precision in diagnosis, which cannot at first sight but be somewhat startling to a mind deeply versed in the knowledge and uncertainties of our art, and to the calm and cautious habits of philosophizing to which the English physician is accustomed.

his work. Laënnec's use of the stethoscope, as well as his exploration of the causes and progression of consumption, ended prematurely when he himself died of the disease in 1826.

Origins of Tubercles?

Laënnec's work concerning the gradual progression of the disease was not followed with much interest until the second half of the century, when researchers were doing a great deal of investigation into the causes of tuberculosis (the term was becoming more popular because of the relationship of the disease to tubercles). One particularly important find was that of another French doctor, Jean-Antoine Villemin, who showed that the disease could be transmitted from a sick animal to a healthy one. Learning what specific thing could make a healthy animal turn sickly would certainly point to the origin of the disease. And with an origin, doctors reasoned, perhaps a cure would not be far behind.

Villemin had served as an army surgeon and had noted certain patterns in the spread of TB among soldiers. He noticed, for example, that troops in the field were less likely to have tuberculosis than were soldiers who had lived for long periods of time in barracks. Among army animals, a similar pattern emerged. Healthy horses that were brought from the country were more likely to develop certain diseases when they were introduced into a large concentration of horses—at an army depot, for instance.

A Carefully Done Experiment

To Villemin in 1865, these observations were fascinating, for they seemed to contradict the current thinking about tuberculosis—that those who contracted it had a certain genetic susceptibility to it. He began a series of experiments, first removing some pus from the lung of a man who had just died of tuberculosis. This he injected into two healthy rabbits. After eight weeks, Villemin noted that the rabbits had both become infected with the disease; their lungs and other organs had become riddled with tubercles.

Encouraged by these results, Villemin continued his experiments, doing six in all. Historians say that he was far more meticulous about his experiments than most scientists of his day. Villemin not only kept detailed records of each step in the process, but also used control subjects—in this case, animals that were not injected with the material from the dead patient. Because these control animals did not become infected with TB, it seemed conclusive that the first animals became sick because of the injections they received.

Over several years, Villemin's experiments showed that he could cause the illness by injecting the animal with one of several materials—the sputum of an infected person, pus from a tubercle, and sometimes even a patient's blood. It was conclusive proof that tuberculosis was contagious and not the result of some inherited weakness or flaw. After all, Villemin maintained, if the disease could be passed from a human to a rabbit or a cow, it certainly could not be hereditary.

But like Laënnec's work in the early 1800s, Villemin's reports went largely ignored. He was politely invited to the prestigious Académie de Médecine in Paris in 1867. However, one historian says that, "his communication was given the most tepid of receptions."[28] Perhaps the reason was that his work had been with rabbits, horses, and cows, rather than humans. At this point in medical history, most doctors were not convinced that findings based on animals were valid in understanding human beings.

Whatever the reason, Villemin was annoyed that the Académie was far more pleased with the speaker who came after him: a professor who claimed to have proved that one's family determined whether a person would contract tuberculosis during his or her lifetime. Understandably, Villemin felt that his hard work had been ignored.

Germs?

Villemin's findings were difficult for many doctors and researchers to accept, for they led to the conclusion that disease was caused by something passing from an infected body to a healthy one. It was, Villemin believed, a kind of germ—too tiny to be seen with the naked eye. And microscopic things such as germs were a controversial idea in Villemin's day.

Antonie van Leeuwenhoek, credited with constructing the first true microscope, had observed tiny living things—called microbes—in 1660. He had been fascinated with the things he saw—an entire world of activity he had never dreamed existed. He drew and wrote about everything he observed—tiny creatures that appeared to reside in so many places, from a drop of pond water to a scraping from his own teeth.

Antonie van Leeuwenhoek, the man credited with inventing the first microscope, observes something through a lens.

That these creatures existed was staggering but easily proven. Anyone with a lens like that Leeuwenhoek had made could see them, and others eagerly did their own experimenting. But where did these creatures come from? And what, if anything, did they do? Those questions divided scientists during Leeuwenhoek's day and continued to divide scientists two centuries later.

A Question Needing an Answer

Some scientists believed that the evidence suggested that microbes, or germs, were at the root of disease. Louis Pasteur had identified germs in spoiled milk, and had found that by heating the milk, he could kill the germs. (This process of killing germs by heating was named pasteurization, after him.) Pasteur strongly believed that most diseases were caused by microbes such as those found in milk. He had written in 1859 that "everything indicates that contagious diseases owe their existence to similar causes."[29]

One who was greatly inspired by Pasteur's work was a German doctor named Robert Koch. As Laënnec had been, he was interested in the process of diseases such as tuberculosis. And while Villemin's experiments showed that tuberculosis could be passed from a sick person to a rabbit or cow, Koch knew that Villemin had not been able to answer the real question: What was the specific cause of tuberculosis? What was it in the blood, sputum, or pus of a person with TB that was able to transmit the disease to a healthy organism?

Robert Koch's Work

Koch suspected, as did many others, that Pasteur's work pointed to a microorganism as the cause of disease. Koch's first experiments were with the blood of a sheep that was infected with another deadly disease called anthrax. He was able to isolate the cause of the disease— in this case, some narrow microorganisms that he noticed in the sheep's blood. To prove these were the cause of anthrax, he injected groups of the organisms into healthy animals, which promptly became ill with anthrax.

Koch wondered if tuberculosis was caused by such an organism. To explore the possibility, he gathered a number of grayish tubercles and crushed them. Looking under a microscope, Koch was disappointed to find nothing at all that looked like a microorganism. He repeated his experiments on other tubercles but was unsuccessful.

Part of the problem, he learned eventually, was the type of dye that many scientists of the day used to highlight various microorganisms—dye that was useless in searching for tiny bacteria such as that which caused tuberculosis. "Not only did the dyes . . . color everything," writes one historian, "making bacteria hard to see; the smears also contained debris that contaminated samples."[30]

"Beautifully Blue"

Koch actually discovered a dye that made the bacillus visible, although his discovery was quite accidental. Medical researchers now know that the bacteria that cause tuberculosis do not stain with dye as easily as other types of bacteria. However, Koch had left a slide with dye on it far longer than he meant to. After several hours, he noticed the forgotten slide and took a quick look under the microscope. What he saw astounded him.

They were, he was certain, the bacteria that he had been trying so hard to see—tiny, rod-shaped microorganisms that were unlike anything he had seen before. Far smaller than the anthrax bacteria, each tuberculosis bacterium—or tubercle bacillus, as he named it—was about 1/25,000 of an inch long. Though small, the bacillus was finally visible, thanks to this unusual dying method. (Koch realized afterward that the dye had worked so well, not only because the slide had sat far longer than normal, but also because it had accidentally come into contact with a chemical in the laboratory—one that he began routinely adding to his TB slides.) As

Robert Koch looks through a microscope in order to study microbes and other minute organisms.

Koch described it later, "Under the microscope all constituents of animal tissue . . . appear faintly brown, with the tubercle bacilli, however, beautifully blue."[31]

Further Proof

Koch was excited by his discovery but wanted absolute proof that this bacillus was indeed the cause of tuberculosis. He decided that to prove this point, he must first separate the bacilli from the tubercle tissue and grow cultures of the bacilli in a pure form. If he could then inject that pure strain of bacillus into healthy animals and have tuberculosis appear as a result, Koch would know for certain that the cause of the disease could be nothing other than the bacillus.

Though the process proved to be difficult, he was able to separate the bacilli from the other matter, and afterward attempted to grow cultures of the microorganisms. Koch believed that observing the behavior of the bacilli under a microscope would be important; observing how they multiplied, grew, and changed would help him understand the bacilli. However, the bacilli did not seem to grow or multiply, unlike other microorganisms Koch had observed, which formed colonies within a day or two.

Nonetheless, Koch was a patient worker. He continued to peer at the cultures each day, hoping to see a change. After almost three weeks, he was elated to see that the bacilli had begun to colonize, just as they must do in the body when a person becomes infected. He dyed sample after sample of the newly grown cultures and observed them under the microscope, and each behaved just as the original microorganisms had.

Announcing His Results

The final proof, however, would be what happened when the bacilli was injected into healthy animals. All Koch's experiments resulted in new cases of tuberculosis in guinea pigs, mice, rats, chickens, and even goldfish. Not satisfied with merely a few good results, Koch tested various cultures over and over, using a total of 230 animals. "Never," writes one researcher, "had there been such a thorough piece of medical investigation."[32]

Koch announced his findings to the medical establishment at the Physiological Society of Berlin on March 24, 1882. He explained that the disease was definitely one that was spread from person to person. He discussed how by breathing the bacillus-infested droplets that infected people created by sneezing or coughing, healthy people could become ill.

Most important, as he told the small gathering, claiming that tuberculosis was some hard-to-define social or genetic ailment was no longer accurate:

Tuberculosis has so far been habitually considered to be a manifestation of social misery, and it has been hoped that an improvement in the latter would reduce the disease. . . . But in future the fight against this terrible plague of mankind will deal no longer with an undetermined something but with a tangible parasite, whose living conditions are for the most part known, and can be investigated further.[33]

Reactions

One might think, given the enormous death toll of tuberculosis at the time, that Koch's announcement would be met with immediate, unanimous cheering. With solid

"Animalculae" and Consumption

One of the first scientific explanations of the germ theory was made in 1722 by a forgotten English doctor named Benjamin Marten. In René and Jean Dubos's book The White Plague: Tuberculosis, Man, and Society, *the authors include an excerpt of Marten's suggestions that "animalculae fretting or gnawing at the vessels of the Stomach, Lungs, Liver" were the cause of consumption—a suggestion made 160 years before Koch actually saw such microorganisms.*

[These factors merely] promote some other Peculiar, Latent or Essential Cause which I suppose to be joined with them. The Original and Essential Cause, then, which some content themselves to call a vicious Disposition of the Juices, others a Salt Acrimony, others a strange Ferment, others a Malignant Humour, may possibly be some certain Species of *Animalculae* or wonderfully minute living creatures that, by their peculiar Shape or disagreeable Parts are inimical to our Nature; but, however, capable of subsisting in our Juices and Vessels. . . .

The minute Animals or their Seed . . . are for the most part either conveyed from Parents to their Offspring hereditarily or communicated immediately from Distempered Persons to sound ones who are very conversant with them. . . . It may, therefore, be very likely that by habitual lying in the same Bed with a consumptive Patient, constantly eating and drinking with him or by very frequently conversing so nearly as to draw in part of the Breath he emits from the lungs, a Consumption may be caught by a sound Person.

scientific proof of the cause of the disease, Koch's words offered hope that doctors might soon gain the upper hand with tuberculosis. After all, researchers had by then developed vaccines for other diseases including smallpox, anthrax, and rabies. Tuberculosis might soon be a thing of the past.

However, the first reaction to Koch's news was varied. In the United States, the medical community seemed uninterested. There was no indication at all of progress in tuberculosis research at an annual American Medical Association convention in St. Paul, Minnesota, held the following May. Writes one historian, no mention of Koch or his experiments was made, "even though the convention began with a ringing paean to science in the keynote address."[34]

Many doctors of the time were skeptical about the real power that bacilli had. They understood that such germs existed, but they were not convinced that they could do as much damage as Koch, Pasteur, and others would have them believe.

"Like a Fairy Tale"

The methods and equipment Koch used in his experiments were also suspect, for outside of a few East Coast medical schools, they were quite uncommon among doctors throughout the United States. Exotic blue dyes and colonies of oddly shaped bacteria seemed mysterious and strange to most of these professionals. One American physician, reading Koch's work for the first time, admitted being filled with wonder at "the ingenuity of the new methods," which, he stated, "read like a fairy tale to me."[35]

Some scientists were eager to duplicate Koch's results, and while a few were successful, others were not as careful in their methods as Koch had been. Their results were less compelling. One scientist wrote two years after Koch's announcement that he had tried to achieve the same results, but he had seen nothing even remotely similar for an entire year. An Austrian scientist claimed to have seen in the healthiest of people such microorganisms that were "indistinguishable from Herr Professor Koch's so-called bacilli."[36]

The press often reflected such resistance. The most influential newspaper in the United States, the *New York Times*, did not even mention Koch's findings until May 5, six weeks after they were announced in Berlin. The newspaper printed a small article about the doctor's experiments with the bacillus. More prominent, however, was an editorial that one expert called "a veiled and rather strange attempt to discredit not only Koch but the whole field of bacteriology."[37]

The editorial was a fictional tale of a ridiculous German character in Wisconsin named Dr. Buhl, who believed that even broken legs were caused by a bacillus. "An ardent believer in the germ theory of nearly all diseases," the editorial explained, "[Dr. Buhl] claims that he has discovered a vegetable parasite which infests the human trousers, [and] maintains . . . that by inoculating human trousers with this parasite after it has been artificially bred in trousers supplied for the purpose to cattle, men will be fully protected against broken legs."[38]

By the 1890s, many doctors were using microscopes as diagnostic tools.

A Gradual Understanding

But while some were initially unconvinced, the next few years saw a gradual understanding of the importance of Koch's discovery. For example, doctors began to acknowledge that the microscope needed to take a more important role in medicine. By the 1890s many doctors were using microscopes as diagnostic tools, routinely inspecting the sputum of patients whom they suspected of having tuberculosis for evidence of the bacillus. One physician noted how important the microscope had recently become, saying that it "was certainly the best friend that a scientist can have. A physician without a microscope is like a man without eyes."[39]

Another noticeable effect of Koch's work was the change in the terminology of the disease. No longer was it referred to as "consumption," as it had been for many years. Now that the cause of it—the tubercle bacillus—had been identified and seen, it could be accurately diagnosed based on the presence of that germ. Who would deny that the correct name was undeniably "tuberculosis?"

Finally, Koch's work gradually added to a newly developing prestige attached to the practice of medicine. Along with discoveries such as the source of anthrax, leprosy, and other diseases, Koch's findings were helping inspire confidence in the science of medicine. There was yet no vaccine for tuberculosis, nor a cure. But it seemed that the battle against the disease was being waged, and science was on the attack.

CHAPTER 3

The Bacillus's Deadly Work

The findings of Robert Koch presented a surprisingly complete picture of the disease that had been responsible for billions of deaths over the centuries. Matched with what has been learned by later research, experts now have a clear idea of how the disease physically affects the body and how it spreads to others.

The Spread of TB

Koch was correct in his explanation of the spread of the tubercle bacilli. "[There] could hardly be any doubt," he explained in his presentation to the medical establishment in Germany, "about the manner by which they get into the air, considering in what excessive numbers tubercle bacilli present in cavity contents are expectorated . . . and are scattered everywhere."[40]

The bacilli are contained in droplets released by the sneezing or coughing of those with tuberculosis. It is also possible to become infected with tuberculosis by eating food contaminated with the bacilli, or by drinking milk from cows with the bovine form of the disease. However, scientists say that the latter form of infection is rare in developed countries like the United States, for all milk that is sold must be pasteurized.

That a droplet from a sneeze or a cough can find its way into the body of another person may seem far-fetched. However, scientists say that one sneeze can

This photograph shows the tiny moisture particles that are expelled when a person sneezes. Thousands of germs can linger in the air after a sneeze.

release 30 million or more droplets into the air—and each one of those droplets can contain as many as one hundred bacilli. The heavier drops almost always fall harmlessly to the ground, say experts. But the light ones—those with only a small amount of fluid—stay airborne. As the moisture evaporates, the bacilli linger in the air, as any piece of dust might.

This is the aspect of tuberculosis that makes it so contagious. A person can breathe in bacilli long after the person who sneezed or coughed has left the room. This easy and unknowing transmission of the disease is extremely worrisome to medical researchers. They remind people that even though a disease such as AIDS (acquired immunodeficiency syndrome) is so frightening, the risk of getting that disease can be lowered by avoiding certain behaviors. But this is not the case with tuberculosis. "Basically, if you don't have sex and are not an IV drug abuser and don't have a blood transfusion," says one British health expert, "there's no other way you can get AIDS. But we've got to breathe."[41]

Settling In

Inhaling the bacilli does not necessarily mean a person will become ill with tuberculosis. The body has defenses that fight off infection. One of these defenses against airborne germs is a layer of thick mucus that covers the entire respiratory system, all the way down to the lungs. The mucus traps bacilli and other foreign particles such as dust or pollen and slowly moves them upward toward the nose and mouth. That mucus can then be spit

The Cough

Although a person with tuberculosis might have a variety of symptoms, the symptom most feared was the cough. As Katherine Ott explains in Fevered Lives: Tuberculosis in American Culture Since 1870, *the tubercular cough had a sound that many found unique.*

[A]n even more fearful symptom was the cough. The cough, rasp, retch, and hack were undeniable tocsins [signs]. O. Henry wrote of a freemasonry [fellowship] among consumptives such that there was no need for introductions: "A cough is your [calling] card; a hemorrhage a letter of credit." An early tuberculosis specialist, Francis Pottenger, vividly recalled the first clear sign of his wife's illness: "On the last day of June, 1895, I heard Carrie cough. It made me shudder. Into my mind flashed the dread word tuberculosis. The fear I endured as I examined her, the feeling of helplessness as we faced the possibility of the same disease which had caused the death of her brother one year before, is indescribable." W. W. Hall described the consumptive's cough for readers of his *Coughs and Colds:* "The fleshless skeleton totters to its pillow, and on the instant, the very instant, the cough begins, at first hard and dry; nothing comes up. Cough, cough, cough! Straining, jarring, racking.". . . William Robertson taught his medical students that the beginning of a consumption was often indicated "with some slight cough, of a dry hacking character, most frequently induced on rising in the morning and going to bed at night . . . at first simply to clear the throat." Just as labored breathing often accompanied cough, so cough slowly progressed from dry and unproductive to expectorative. Patients and physicians endlessly studied sputum brought up and deposited in cups, handkerchiefs, enameled bowls, and upon the floor.

out, blown out into a tissue, or even swallowed. (In the latter case, it will pass easily through the digestive system, doing no harm.) This mucus, which is brought forth from the lungs, is what is known as sputum.

However, some bacilli may get past the defense systems. Sometimes they are breathed deeply into the lungs, into little air sacs called alveoli. If bacilli get to the alveoli, they can sometimes cause what doctors call a "primary infection." This is a stage of tuberculosis, but it does not necessarily mean that the person will actually get the disease.

Meeting the Macrophages

Once an invading germ gets to the alveoli, it is singled out for attack by white blood cells called macrophages, whose job is to wipe out any dangerous invader before it can do harm to the body. "These cells are really amazing," says medical research technician Jim Steele. "One of my biology professors used to call them Pacman cells [a reference to a popular arcade game of the 1980s]. Anytime there's an intruder, a possible enemy within the body, these cells eat the bacteria and digest it."[42]

Only a few years after Koch's discovery of the tuberculosis bacillus, scientists began understanding the workings of white blood cells such as macrophages. They learned that in most cases of infection, a chemical reaction occurs, triggering the bone marrow to produce more of the cells than usual—a million times more, in fact.

Within minutes of this chemical alert, writes researcher Thomas Dormandy, "billions of them, some obviously hastily assembled and only half-finished, [are] carried by the bloodstream to the site of the invasion."[43] Once there, they began ingesting the invading microorganisms. However, experts have learned that this process changes when the invaders are tuberculosis bacilli.

A System Gone Haywire

When a tuberculosis germ enters the body and penetrates as deep as the alveoli, the chemical response is not

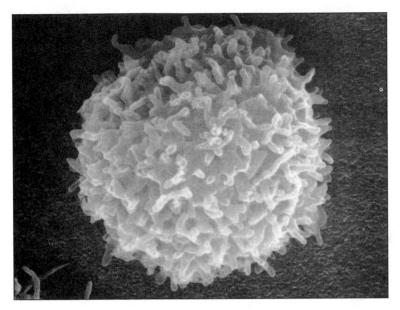

Macrophages, or white blood cells, act as the body's defense to destroy invading germs.

the same. The numbers of macrophages are much smaller, and they do not rush to the site of the bacteria, as they do with other infections. Scientists are still unsure why the bone marrow does not produce more macrophages when TB germs are present.

When the macrophages do reach the TB bacilli, they ingest the invaders, as they do in other instances. But they are unable to digest the bacilli. Modern scientists have found that the reason the cells are unable to digest TB germs is the amazingly thick coating on the surface of the bacilli, which, says one researcher, is as about as tough as "a steel-belted radial."[44]

Ironically, not only are the macrophages unable to digest the invaders, but somehow the interior of the cells proves to be the perfect environment for the bacilli to multiply. Some of the bloated macrophages (the TB germs still within them) drift up to the mucus-lined walls of the lungs and are eventually expelled as sputum. However, other macrophages become clumped together with their continually growing load of bacilli. They are joined by other white blood cells, who attempt to fight the bacilli. Unfortunately, the germs apparently cannot be destroyed.

A Primary Infection

Soon, within the alveoli appears a little mass of cells—the bacilli-laden macrophages surrounded by other cells. Within ten days to two weeks, the mass changes to a hard gray or pinkish lump—the bacilli still trapped deep inside. This is what the seventeenth-century scientist Sylvius had first observed and named a "tubercle."

As time goes by, the tubercle may increase in size, and when it does, nearby lung tissue is destroyed. Within the tubercle, some of the macrophages and other white cells gradually die, and their residue forms the cheesy, soft areas that Sylvius had observed. The body's defenses attempt to keep the tubercle isolated by forming scar tissue around it to slow or halt its multiplying. When the scar tissue surrounds it, the tubercle is trapped—and is, for the time being, harmless.

The bacilli within the tubercle do not die, however. They are inactive, and the person is said to have a primary infection. This does not mean that the person has tuberculosis. In fact, many people with primary infections never get tuberculosis. Explains one researcher, "Only one infected person in ten actually develops the disease. . . . The other nine battle the microbe to an immunological stalemate."[45]

Many who have a primary infection in their lungs have no symptoms. Occasionally a person may get a slight rash or a low-grade fever. These symptoms are almost never severe enough for a person to seek medical attention. Because of this, a person with a primary infection may never realize he or she has been infected.

The One Case in Ten

How does a person actually become sick with tuberculosis? The only way this can occur is when the bacilli contained within the tubercle become active. Full-blown tuberculosis can develop quickly, especially if the person is a child or an elderly person, or has another illness. But in most people who have inactive tubercles, the disease does not develop for decades. "TB is very, very persistent," says John McKinney, director of Rockefeller University's Laboratory of Infection Biology. "A person infected sixty years ago could still harbor the bug."[46]

No one is certain exactly what triggers the bacilli to become active once more. Most researchers believe that the body's defenses are the key, however. When they are overtaxed or are simply inadequate for some reason, the tubercles rupture and bacilli begin multiplying once again. And although the tuberculosis bacilli reproduce at a far slower rate than other germs—every twelve to twenty hours, as compared with every twenty minutes or so—the new bacilli quickly create more tubercles, which further damage the lungs.

As they multiply and take advantage of the body's inability to adequately defend itself, the bacilli are carried to other parts of the lung, to the lymph vessels. The germs, which are often still within the macrophage, may also be carried along in the blood vessels. This is dangerous, for it spreads the disease to other organs, such as the skin, the kidneys, and the bones. The bacilli have the capability of infecting every part of the human body, says one medical expert, "from liver to brain, from the fingertips to the delicate structures of our eyes."[47]

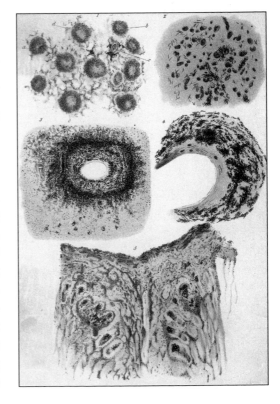

These cells are infected with tubercle bacilli.

Deadly Symptoms

This stage is called active tuberculosis, and the symptoms can be far more acute than in the primary infection stage. When the infection becomes reactivated, the person may have a dry, persistent cough or a lack of energy. Some may have chest pains or difficulty breathing when climbing stairs or running. But because some of these symptoms may also mean a lingering cold, a bout of bronchitis, or simple fatigue, it is not difficult to understand why many patients simply wait for the symptoms to go away on their own.

In the second stage of tuberculosis, the symptoms are more alarming. As more and more of the cells in the lung (or other infection site) continue to damage the tissue, more and more of the cheeselike material replaces it. This material can become more liquid, and as it irritates the respiratory system, the person coughs it up as sputum. In only a matter of time, the lung simply dissolves, for the material, when coughed up, leaves holes—called lesions—in the lung tissue.

These lesions, say experts, are fertile breeding grounds for the ever-increasing bacilli. A single lesion may contain as many as 10 billion bacilli, which can quickly destroy the entire lung. One visitor to a Russian prison, where tuberculosis is rampant, recalls wincing when he looked at a patient's chest X ray. "There has been a marked enlargement of the [lesions] in Sergei's right lung," he wrote. "Spreading inexorably, tubercle bacilli have already reduced half of that lung to Swiss cheese." [48]

"It Is My Death Warrant"

Examining sputum samples can reveal a great deal about the course of a patient's tuberculosis. Many years before Koch's findings about the cause of tuberculosis, physicians were carefully checking the smell, appearance, and texture of the material brought up from the lungs. One nineteenth-century physician took careful note of the amount of sputum his patients brought up, and claimed he had a few patients who might in a few weeks cough up more than their own weight in the substance.

Without a doubt, the most alarming sign in sputum has always been bright red blood. This occurs when blood vessels in the lungs become damaged by the bacilli. In many cases, blood is the symptom that signals the sufferer to seek medical attention, for his or her ailment is more than a simple case of bronchitis. In the nineteenth century, the presence of blood was alarming in the same way that a breast lump is today.

In the winter of 1818, the poet John Keats had been feeling somewhat unwell for a short time. A friend later recalled the exact moment Keats realized the seriousness of his condition:

> On entering the cold sheets, before his head was on the pillow, he coughed and I heard him say—"This is blood." I approached him and saw that he was examining a stain on the sheet. "Bring me a candle, Brown, and let me see this blood." After I handed him the candle and he examined the blood he looked up in my face with a calmness of countenance that I can never forget and said: "This is arterial blood: I cannot be deceived by its color. It is my death warrant.[49]

Poet John Keats (pictured) was a victim of TB in the nineteenth century.

The Final Stage

Death may come very quickly if a lesion is at the site of a major artery in the lung, for the patient may bleed to death while coughing, literally drowning in his or her own blood. If the bleeding is less severe, the disease will continue to worsen at a slow pace. Breathing becomes labored and chest pain is more severe.

The patient loses weight, too, and has almost no appetite. A fever occurs each day about the same time and usually spikes during the afternoon; at night the fever produces night sweats. These episodes are often so acute, say doctors, that a patient may need to have his or her pajamas and sheets changed several times in one night.

Even before Koch's discovery of the bacillus at the end of the nineteenth century, doctors knew by the time such symptoms presented themselves that the patient was close to death. Doctors were frustrated to realize there was little they could do, other than try to make the patient a bit more comfortable as the disease progressed. The medical community hoped that with the new knowledge Koch had shared, some cure might be found. And, the hope was, that it would happen quickly, before too many more would die.

"A New Potent Hope"

In 1890 it seemed for a time that Koch himself might have found the cure. In a presentation before the Tenth International Congress of Medicine in Berlin, Koch announced that he had discovered a substance, which he called tuberculin, that could protect people against TB—and in some cases, even cure the disease once someone was infected with it.

Not surprisingly, the news caused great excitement throughout the world. One journalist reported, "The consumptive patients of the Continent have been stampeding for dear life for the capital of Germany. The dying have hurried thither, sometimes to expire in the railway train, but buoyed up for a time by a new potent hope."[50] Another newspaper in the Mediterranean Riviera stated:

A man is inoculated with Robert Koch's supposed cure for tuberculosis, which turned out to have no effect.

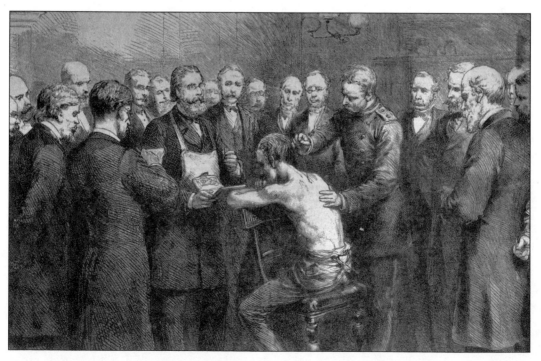

The whole community was moved to meet [Koch]. His fame went throughout the region around about, and telegrams in the newspapers announced that all the sleeping cars had been engaged for months to come to convey the consumptives of the Riviera to the inclement latitude of Berlin. [51]

Disappointment

But their joy was short-lived. Much to Koch's dismay, tuberculin, which was made up of a sterile form of the bacillus, did not cure or prevent tuberculosis after all.

Why?

When Robert Koch announced in 1890 at the Tenth International Congress of Medicine in Berlin that he had found a substance that could, in some instances, protect against TB and even perhaps cure the disease, it set off an electrifying response. The reaction was not surprising, considering that TB was virtually an epidemic.

What was surprising, however, was that Koch's "vaccine" was quickly found to be useless in curing or preventing TB—and in many cases, actually hastened the death of those with the disease. Such an outrageous claim might have been chalked up to a lesser scientist, or to one of the scam artists selling magic potions for TB at county fairs across the United States. But Koch, the man who had gained such international renown just eighteen years earlier by his discovery of the tubercle bacillus? People were appalled and could not understand what had prompted a man known for his conservative, methodical approach to experiments to be so careless.

Koch never gave an explanation or expressed a public reaction, other than surprise at the dismal results of tuberculin in TB patients. In Berlin alone, over two thousand patients were treated with tuberculin, and they died at a rate far above the rate for TB patients who had not been treated at all. Today, the most prevalent explanation for Koch's haste in introducing tuberculin is a most unflattering one—that he and the Prussian government had made a secret agreement to split the profits made in worldwide sales of the formula. One thing was sure: The prestige and respect Koch had attained in 1882 were diminished by the tuberculin episode.

"Those Naughty, Naughty Roentgen Rays"

Just after Robert Koch's announcement of a vaccine for TB was found to be false, a very important discovery was made in Germany by a professor of physics, Wilhelm Conrad Röntgen. While Röntgen's X-ray apparatus would not cure or prevent tuberculosis, it would prove to be an amazing diagnostic tool, as Thomas Dormandy explains in this excerpt from The White Death: A History of Tuberculosis.

On the night of 8 November 1895 . . . Röntgen . . . was completing a routine investigation into phenomena accompanying the passage of an electric current through a vacuum tube. The laboratory was in darkness and the tube was enveloped in black cardboard. Since this was supposed to make it impervious to light, Röntgen was surprised to notice that a few crystals left by accident on the bench some distance away became brilliantly illuminated. He placed them at a greater distance and still they fluoresced. Then he placed materials of varying density between his vacuum tube and the crystals. First he used a book, then a piece of timber, then glass, then various metal objects; and he found that to a lesser or greater degree all were transparent to the newly discovered rays. . . .

Röntgen christened the new rays "X-rays," and announced his discovery to the Wurzburg Medical Society on 28 December 1895. Within a few months his paper was translated into several languages and . . . was immediately hailed as revolutionary. Indeed, it created a sensation among the lay public as much as it did in medical circles: a London clothing firm soon advertised "X-ray-proof underclothing for ladies" and Miss Marie Lloyd [a popular singer of the day] immortally sang:

"I'm full of daze
Shock and amaze
For nowadays
I hear they'll gaze
Through cloak and gown and even stays
Those naughty, naughty Roentgen rays."

Chest X-rays and their lineal successor were to transform the diagnosis of tuberculosis; and the mass X-ray was to become the first and arguably still the most successful screening programme in preventative medicine.

Pictured is Wilhelm Röntgen, the discoverer of X rays, a development that led to the first successful medical diagnostic tool.

Results he had achieved with laboratory animals were not duplicated in human patients. In some cases, the treatment even seemed to increase and accelerate the deaths. Within months, Koch was vilified in the press, criticized as unethical and rash.

The question of how a scientist so well known for his conservative, careful work would have made such claims before being certain of his results is still unanswered. Some historians claim the German government was unfairly pressuring Koch to find a quick cure, while others say he was distracted because of a crumbling marriage.

Whatever the reason, Koch's tuberculin was a failure as a cure or vaccine. However, it was eventually found to be very valuable as a diagnostic tool. By injecting a tiny bit of tuberculin under a person's skin, a doctor could determine whether that patient had ever been infected with TB. A person who is exposed to tuberculosis creates antibodies, which attempt to fight the disease. The tuberculin interacts with those antibodies, which cause the site of the injection to turn red and bumpy. Koch's tuberculin was developed further by Charles Mantoux; the Mantoux test is given to most people today as part of a routine physical examination.

But a diagnostic tool is not a cure. As the nineteenth century drew to an end, doctors knew a great deal about the progression and spread of tuberculosis. They had become more efficient at diagnosing it, too. However, once the disease was diagnosed, the prognosis was still grim.

Chapter 4

Going on the Offensive

Robert Koch's inability to come up with either a vaccine or a cure for tuberculosis was disappointing. However, in the years following Koch's discovery of the bacillus, others proposed new ideas for dealing with tuberculosis. Some attempted to find cures for those dying of the disease; others proposed ideas aimed instead at reducing the numbers of new cases.

A Disease of the Masses

After Koch proved that tuberculosis was caused by a microscopic germ and was therefore contagious, public health officials turned their attention to those people most at risk for contracting the disease. The urban poor—especially the immigrants who lived in the most crowded tenement houses—were the likeliest segment of society to become infected.

In New York City, for example, tuberculosis accounted for 390 of every 100,000 deaths. However, when the statisticians looked more carefully at each district of the city, they found that the wealthy areas had very low TB rates. On the upper West Side, for instance, the death rate was only 49 of every 100,000 deaths. But in the crowded neighborhoods of lower Manhattan, TB accounted for 776 of every 100,000 deaths.

Such statistics indicated that the poor were becoming ill and dying at a much faster rate than those who were better off financially. No doubt, said the public health officials, the cramped conditions, poor diet, and lack of understanding about how germs are passed from person to person were responsible for the vast difference between the TB statistics of rich and poor.

There were no thoughts of ignoring the problem, for sick workers among the poor were a threat to everyone; having money did not protect a person from becoming infected from a cook, a maid, a baker, or any other person who coughed up tuberculoid-filled sputum. The problem needed to be dealt with—the sooner the better.

Declaring War on Tuberculosis

In the United States, organization seemed the best way to fight the problem. Dr. Hermann Biggs of the New York City Department of Health claimed that amazing things could happen if society addressed itself to merely stop the chain of infection a little at a time. He told the Philadelphia County Medical Society in 1900:

A woman sits with her baby in a run-down tenement room. Tuberculosis was a serious epidemic in poor residential areas like this.

While no one would assume that in a single month or in a single year all of the thousands and tens of thousands of sources of infection in a great city can be removed, yet if one-quarter or one-third can be eradicated there will be a proportionate gain, which will be increased each succeeding year.[52]

Health workers and other volunteers all over the nation began forming anti-tuberculosis leagues in their own cities and towns. They distributed pamphlets explaining how the disease was spread. They created signs reminding people to wash their hands frequently, to eat healthy meals, and to get plenty of fresh air. The bacillus, they explained, was less likely to infect someone who had good health habits to begin with.

The leagues also employed some more grisly techniques in educating the public about tuberculosis. They created "Anti-Tuberculosis Health Exhibits," which were displayed in local saloons. The exhibits almost always featured a jar containing one or two tuberculous human lungs preserved in formaldehyde, as well as a large, painted skeleton whose eyes would flash every few minutes to signal another death by TB in the United States.

Spitting, Pencils, and Hotel Blankets

In many cities throughout the United States, women volunteers plastered signs on shop windows and restaurants admonishing men to stop spitting—a habit, writes one historian, that was considered "the worst of the mortal sins."[53] The tubercle, these advocates insisted, was in every droplet of spit, by the millions. And even when the spit on the street dried, people could still tread on it, and the germs would then be brought into their homes. To make their point, these anti-tuberculosis league members, armed with buckets and mops, scrubbed sidewalks and street corners.

But spitting was only one of many behaviors that had to change to reduce the spread of tuberculosis, according to the leagues. The list of dos and don'ts seemed endless;

"Selling the Anti-Tuberculosis Message"

One of the ways in which the anti-tuberculosis leagues gathered public support was to advertise—in essence, marketing their message that germs caused tuberculosis. In her book, The Gospel of Germs: Men, Women, and the Microbe in American Life, *Nancy Tomes describes some of the more successful campaigns.*

At the simplest level, the new advertising taught the virtue of the well-chosen phrase, or "jingle"—for example, Schlitz's tag "the beer that made Milwaukee famous" or Kodak's slogan, "You push the button, we do the rest." Although tuberculosis did not lend itself so easily to jingle making, the basic principle of writing advertising copy—make the message short and memorable—worked equally well in health education. Imitating the advertisement, tuberculosis workers sought to compress their preventive gospel into brief slogans or mottos, such as "Don't spit," "Fresh air promotes health," and "Flies carry disease." The layout of educational materials was also changed to make the slogans easier to read at a glance. The slogan style was particularly well adapted for display advertising in newspapers, streetcars, and billboards; in Topeka, Kansas, even the sidewalks were put to use by being laid with bricks that read "Don't Spit."

Anti-TB societies also exploited the concept of the trademark, which companies such as Procter and Gamble and Quaker Oats had developed in the late nineteenth century to distinguish their supposedly superior wares from cheaper, generic brands. In 1906, the NTA [National Tuberculosis Association] adopted the double barred Lorraine cross as its symbol in order to distance itself from competitors in the White Cross League, which sold toilet articles to raise money for consumptives. The Lorraine cross [still used today on Christmas seals] lent itself well to display advertising and became a focal point in all of the NTA's publicity campaigns.

there were strict rules on nose blowing, setting a table, decorating a room, and planning a vacation. One pamphlet warned that, to avoid catching the TB germ from a contaminated blanket in a hotel room, "[t]he careful traveller will . . . insist that the blanket be covered by a fresh clean sheet the turn down of which shall cover it for a distance of two feet from the top."[54]

Any pencil was to be avoided, since a person with tuberculosis might have recently handled it. The leagues also created strict rules concerning money, drinking cups, and the seats of trains. And lest anyone doubt the necessity of such rules, one often-quoted league pamphlet began with the warning: "We are each one of us in hourly danger."[55]

Attacking the Source

Besides educating the public about general principles of healthy living, some anti-tuberculosis leagues tried to tackle the cause of the problem—in this case, the poverty in which most sufferers lived. League members wrote pamphlets about poor housing and the long, grueling hours spent working in unsafe conditions. They pointed out that poor people could barely afford heat and warm clothes, and failed to eat well-balanced meals.

A volunteer from one of the many anti-tuberculosis leagues uses a poster to help teach a family about cleaner and safer living conditions.

In 1913, the Cincinnati league even produced a film called *Darkest Cincinnati*, which showed wealthier audiences the living conditions in the city's slums. "Scene Five" announces a narrator early in the film. "A court between 4th and 5th streets. A Sunday view of a court in this neighborhood. Filth and garbage from end to end. The stench is awful. Note the little girls carrying babies in their arms over piles of rotten garbage."[56]

The anti-tuberculosis leagues raised public awareness about the problems of overcrowding, of child labor, and other aspects of poverty in American cities. However, blame began to shift from the conditions of the poor to the poor themselves. Leaders of various leagues often sounded more than a little hostile toward the sick people they started out trying to help.

"Weak, Shiftless, Lacking in Initiative"

Perhaps one reason for such hostility was fear; because the poor were the most likely to carry the germs, the public began to perceive them as menaces to society. After all, the reasoning went, if much of the spreading of germs could be avoided by better hygiene, then weren't those who continued to live in filthy homes and crowded tenements simply lazy?

Many in the anti-tuberculosis leagues supported that view. Ellen La Motte, a vocal anti-tuberculosis league leader, claimed that the poor who lived in such conditions "are by nature weak, shiftless, lacking in initiative and perseverance. They have neither inherited nor acquired moral strength . . . and are often vicious besides."[57]

Those with tuberculosis were to be helped, but with a sometimes unfriendly sort of charity. Racial and cultural stereotypes were used to explain why black, Native American, and Irish people were far more likely to be infected. "Lungers," as the infected poor were often called, were described more and more with adjectives such as "careless" and "unteachable," and were assumed to be uneducated and foreign-born.

One outspoken public health nurse wrote in 1909 of the difference in teaching the public ways to avoid catching

tuberculosis. Much of society could learn what they needed to protect themselves and their families, she explained,
but "the day laborer, the shop girl, the drunken negro
belong to a class which, *by reason of the very conditions which
constitute it as a class,* is unable to make use of what it
learns."[58]

Rules for the Sick

By referring to tuberculosis sufferers in these kinds of
terms, it was easier to take the next step—enacting laws
and rules that would limit what people with the disease
were allowed to do. At New York City's board of health,
Hermann Biggs had accomplished a great deal—in
pressing for better education about TB and advocating
the disinfecting of hospital rooms used by patients with
the disease. Realizing that these measures were not
enough, Biggs became a leading advocate for the mandatory registration of all people with tuberculosis. New
York physicians in 1897 were advised to supply the board
of health with the names and addresses of all patients
who had been diagnosed with TB. Within a decade,
eighty-four other cities had followed New York's lead.

The requirement was not a popular one. Doctors
resented it because it caused them to violate the confi-
dentiality of the doctor–patient relationship. They also
feared that their patients would be nervous about seeking treatment if they knew their names would appear in
official logs. Patients worried that they would lose insurance benefits, or even their jobs, if their employers knew
about their disease.

And while public opinion differed about the government's role in the personal lives of citizens, Biggs and
other leaders defended their actions as necessary for the
welfare of the healthy public. "The government of the
United States is democratic," he insisted. "But the sanitary measures adopted are sometimes autocratic, and
the functions performed by sanitary authorities paternal
in character. We are prepared, when necessary, to intro-
duce and enforce . . . measures which might seem radi-

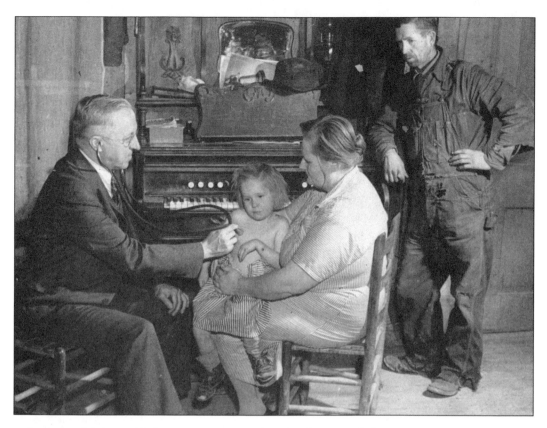

A doctor examines a child in a rural farmhouse in the 1940s.

cal and arbitrary, if they were not plainly designed for the public good."[59]

Stricter Rules

The consequences of the mandatory reporting of TB cases were worse than critics of the plan had predicted. Around the United States, landlords refused to rent to anyone whose name appeared on the rolls. Insurance companies—realizing that the disease almost always resulted in death—either canceled the policies of people suffering from TB, or else added a clause stating they would not pay for any tuberculosis-related claims.

Many states passed laws that banned infected people from working in certain places, such as dairies, restaurants, or bakeries—no matter how good their precautions were. Some states even barred people with tuberculosis from teaching school, though these laws

"The Deliberate Creation of a Pesthouse"

A diagnosis of tuberculosis not only affected a patient's health, but also had the ability in the early twentieth century to force people to cancel plans to marry and start a family, as historian Katherine Ott explains in her book, Fevered Lives: Tuberculosis in American Culture Since 1870.

[Tuberculosis] was added to the list of eugenic defects that could disqualify couples from marrying. Physicians believed they had a responsibility to both the community and their patients to counsel against consumptives marrying. As one doctor put it, "Marriage of Consumptives is often the deliberate creation of a pesthouse." Washington State had a law forbidding those with advanced tuberculosis from marrying, under penalty of a $1,000 fine and three years in jail. Those who supported eugenic theory [the idea that by controlled selective breeding, the human race could be improved] counseled patients not to marry if there was a predisposition to [TB] in their families. They advised tubercular women who were already married to avoid pregnancy, lest they produce defective offspring. A resident of De Tour, Michigan, wrote to the editor of *Everybody's Magazine:* "It is inhuman, it is outrageous and next to murder for consumptives to bring children into the world." Charles Davenport, an outspoken eugenicist who was hypervigilant about the white middle-class gene pool, recommended that physicians issue certificates for tuberculosis purity.

were eventually repealed after World War II, when medications that were effective against TB were found.

An especially emotional battle took place over the issue of restricting interstate travel. Especially in California, where the climate of warm weather and sunshine was far friendlier for those with tuberculosis than northern states, tempers flared. One California doctor was furious that people with TB were entering his state. "Why should this glorious State be stocked with consumptives and their offspring?" he complained. "Instead of this State producing a people with mental and bodily vigor . . . we shall have a race weak in mind and body, and deeply tainted with a predisposition to consumption."[60] Others shared his concerns, but banning entry proved to be impossible. Even those who were afraid of catching tuberculosis from one of the imported "lungers" realized how impractical it would be to patrol the state's borders.

Those who were more sympathetic to the needs of the sick pleaded with others to remember that anyone rich, or poor, could catch tuberculosis. "The society which would add unnecessary stigma to them," one public health official warned, "is culpable and inhumane."[61]

Edward Trudeau

During the same time that Hermann Biggs and others were dealing with the politics of tuberculosis, an interesting medical experiment was in progress. It was orchestrated by a young doctor, Edward Livingston Trudeau, who had become ill with tuberculosis after tending to his brother who had been dying of the disease.

As Trudeau's health failed, he decided to visit the Adirondack Mountains, a place he had always loved. If he was to die, he would rather die there. "If I had but a short time to live I yearned for surroundings that appealed to me," he wrote later, "and it seemed to meet a longing I had for rest and the peace of the great wilderness."[62] Though he was faint and burning with fever, he spent the summer in the fresh air and sunshine.

To his great suprise, Trudeau gained weight and felt much better. He returned to the city but soon began feeling ill. When he went back to the mountains for a second time, he noted, "Little by little, while lying out uder the great trees, looking out on the lake all day, my fever has stopped and my health slowly begun to return."[63]

The Sanatorium

Hoping that others suffering from TB could be helped in the same way, Trudeau decided to open a health resort in the Saranac Lakes region of northern New York. It would allow people with the disease to get away from the cities where they lived, to a simpler, more healthful environment. This sanatorium, or retreat, opened in 1848.

Trudeau's sanatorium was the first in the United States, but facilities like it had been operating for years in Europe. Not really hospitals, European sanitoriums were places where upper-class people with TB could rest, eat good, wholesome food, and perhaps regain their strength. Ironically, European sanatoriums were losing popularity just as Trudeau's Saranac Lake sanatorium was in its planning stages.

Saranac Lake was different; what Trudeau wanted was a sanatorium not for rich people but for the poor whose choices were limited. And in return for free care at Saranac Lake, the patients would test his theory that

"The World Had Grown Suddenly Dark"

In An Autobiography, *Edward Trudeau recounts the day he was diagnosed with tuberculosis. After experiencing fatigue, fever, and swollen lymph nodes, he agreed to have a physical examination. Afterward, he says, he was curious why the doctor seemed so quiet.*

"Well, Dr. Janeway, you can find nothing the matter?" He looked grave and said, "Yes, the upper two-thirds of the left lung is involved in an active tuberculosis process."

I think I know something of the feelings of the man at the bar who is told he is to be hanged on a given date, for in those days pulmonary tuberculosis was considered absolutely fatal. I pulled myself together, put as good a face on the matter as I could, and escaped from the office after thanking the doctor for his examination. When I got outside . . . I felt stunned. It seemed to me the world had grown suddenly dark. The sun was shining, it is true, and the street was filled with the rush and noise of brightness. I had consumption—that most fatal of diseases! Had I not seen it in all its horrors in my brother's case? It meant death and I had never thought of death before! Was I ready to die? How could I tell my wife, whom I had just left in unconscious happiness with the little baby in our new home? And my rose-colored dreams of achievement and professional success in New York! They were all shattered now, and in their place only exile and the inevitable end remained!

life in such a setting could improve the health of those with TB. Since these patients could not afford to pay the exorbitant rates charged at European sanatoriums, Trudeau appealed to churches, foundations, and wealthy investors for money to run his facility.

Such fund-raising was not often easy, Trudeau admitted, for TB was a disease that people knew was almost always fatal. "Many people argued," he wrote, "that it was well known that tuberculosis could not be cured . . . that an aggregation of dying invalids would be so depressing that nobody would want to stay . . . that the climate was rough."[64] Still, he remained persuasive—living proof that the right surroundings could work magic on a person who had been near death only months before.

Life at Saranac Lake

Trudeau tried to recruit patients who were in the early stages of tuberculosis, for he thought he would have a better chance of reversing their disease. Trudeau explained that the two most important aspects of care at Saranac Lake were eating and living an outdoor life. Patients were fed a rich diet—three meals a day and a glass of milk every four hours. And each patient was urged to slowly become used to spending eight to ten hours outdoors each day.

Trudeau visited patients each day, moving through the rooms and the airy, bright porches where the sick lay bundled in robes. He always wore his hunting clothes because he felt they reflected his outdoorsy way of life. Even after white coats became the standard uniform for a doctor, writes one historian, "Trudeau refused to discard the knickerbockers and leather leggins of hunting days."[65]

He and his staff expected discipline and good manners from the patients, as he explained to them firmly. Patients were required to keep their rooms neat and orderly, and to be respectful to the staff and other patients. They were constantly reminded about the correct way to rid themselves of sputum. Trudeau provided spittoons and warned that anyone who spit anywhere else would be sent home.

Some patients did feel stronger after their stay at Saranac Lake and eventually returned to their homes. After a few years, the facility was opened to wealthy and middle-class patients, as well. The sanatorium had been much talked about, and many were eager to see what the outdoor life could do for them. Though it is not clear how many patients were completely cured (even Trudeau's TB returned years later), about one-third of Trudeau's patients said they felt better.

Many Varieties

Trudeau's idea was soon adopted by other doctors who established their own sanatoriums. Fifty years after the founding of Saranac Lake sanatorium, there were six hundred new facilities around the country, with a combined capacity of over ninety-five thousand beds. Some followed Trudeau's regimen, while others varied in their approaches.

For instance, while patients at Saranac Lake were urged to become more active by hiking, fishing, and taking part in other forms of exercise, some sanatorium directors thought that sitting outside in fresh air was enough. Rest, they insisted, was far more helpful than exercise.

Some patients commented that a sanatorium could make the idea of resting sound exhausting, for there were so many rules for doing it correctly. "You are not relaxed," warned a rule book at the Mount McGregor Sanatorium, "if you lie with your arms behind your head, read, or listen to the radio."[66] Another rule book detailed guidelines for bundling up in a rug to relax on a deck chair outside:

> Place the rug, which should be large in size, fully extended on the chair. After sitting down, grasp the part of the rug lying on the right of the chair and with a quick motion, throw it over the feet and knees and tuck it well under the legs. Then do the same with the part of the rug on the other

side of the chair, but leave the edge free. Now grasp the free edge of the rug lying on the right hand side and pull it up hand over hand until the end . . . is reached. Then pull up the far end of the rug, taking care to uncover as little as possible of the legs but only one over the feet. It forms, however, a bag out of the rug and no air can enter.[67]

At this TB sanatorium in the mountains of Colorado, each patient had a separate cottage.

Guidelines for what and how much to eat also varied from facility to facility. Some physicians claimed that it was important to keep meals healthful but small; others insisted that a patient should eat as much as possible. "It is an old adage among patients of tuberculosis," wrote one doctor, "that they should eat once for themselves, once for the germs, and once to gain weight."[68]

"Be a Bright Blue"

Almost all of the sanatoriums shared some ideas, however. One of the most important was a need for optimism—by doctors, nurses, and especially the patients themselves. Most sanatorium workers believed a positive attitude to be a key factor in regaining health.

Because tension and pessimism were thought to bring on sickness and depression, patients were forbidden to talk about their illness at most facilities.

Finances, patients' jobs (or lack of jobs), and relationships with friends and families were topics that tended to promote worry; instead patients were advised to concentrate on the task nearest at hand—getting well.

Patients found only cheerful, upbeat reading material available to them, and signs with pleasant pictures or optimistic maxims were on every wall. Author Betty MacDonald, who was a patient in a Seattle sanatorium in the 1930s, remembers that meals were always served with a little card printed with a cheerful saying, such as, "If you must be blue [sad], be a bright blue."[69]

Nighttime at the Sanatorium

Author Betty MacDonald spent time in a Seattle sanatorium for her tuberculosis in the 1930s and found that the place lost its optimistic aura at night—becoming eerie and foreboding. This remembrance of MacDonald's is included in Mark Caldwell's The Last Crusade: The War on Consumption, 1862–1954.

I awoke in the cold, early night to the dark stillness of the ward. I always hated the Pines at night. It was so much a hospital where anything might happen, anyone might die. . . . The Barking Dog [one of the patients] began to cough, her coughs bursting from her like balls from a Roman candle. She coughed twenty-two times, then drank water and put the glass back on the stand with a clink. The woman across from her coughed, drank water, and coughed again. . . . Finally everyone seemed to be awake and there were coughs up and down the halls like a relay race. A grim terrible race with Death holding the stakes. I thought of Eileen cold and alone with sandbags on her chest. Sylvia had said that hemorrhages were very frightening. That the blood was bright red and foamy.

Someone was tapping on her stand. It was the way to summon a nurse but never used, especially at night, except in an emergency. The tapping went on, clink, clink, clink, clink. It seemed to come from down the hall where the private rooms were. Eleanor said in a whisper, "Something's happened. I hear a doctor." . . .

Morning came at last, dark and wild with wind and rain lashing and clawing at the windows. The ward was oppressively quiet. The day staff came on duty, cheerful and brisk, bringing breakfast. I gulped down two cups of warm, comforting coffee but I couldn't shake the horror of the night before. I . . . thought I detected an ominous undercurrent. . . . In the bathroom I learned, from one of the older patients, that a girl in emergency had died during the night. I had never seen the girl, didn't even know her name but it was my first death. My slowly built up confidence and assurance of recovery were kicked from under me, I shivered uncontrollably. . . .

Order Within Chaos

But the most vital aspect of the tuberculosis sanatorium was its ceaseless regimentation. Rules were everywhere; all patients were handed a rule book after checking in, and lest they forget any of the rules, staff members reminded them every day. More things were forbidden than allowed, some patients laughed. The rule book was the bible, agrees one historian: "It told you when to get up, when to brush your teeth, how to brush your teeth, when and how to talk, how to cover your mouth when you coughed, and even how much you could read."[70]

Schedules were created for everything, and doctors and other staff personnel made certain that they were followed to the minute. The reason for the abundance of rules was the disease itself. An incurable disease such as tuberculosis was, according to historian Ken Chowder, a kind of social chaos, in which nothing made sense. The sanatorium was medicine's way of trying to instill order. Explains Chowder, "The restrictive rules can be seen as an attempt to give the illusion of human control over a disease that was in fact uncontrollable."[71]

The uncontrollable nature of the disease was proving more and more frustrating to doctors and their patients. The fear of catching TB remained a concern, even though many doctors tried to reassure the public that such fear was out of proportion to the real threat of contagion. Historians note that the fear of catching TB was as irrational as the fear of contracting AIDS can be today. Barbers refused to shave consumptive men. Some employers fired anyone with TB, no matter how attentive the worker was to personal hygiene. Misinformation seemed to win out over medical sense; the public fear was far out of proportion to the real threat of contagion. "It almost seemed," writes one researcher of the period, "as if tuberculosis had been specially created to test national and personal character."[72] With every decade that passed, the fear of tuberculosis became more intense, putting an unbecoming taint on that national character.

Chapter 5

Winning and Losing

Early in the twentieth century, the outlook for a tuberculosis cure still seemed bleak. As a diagnosis of the disease continued to amount to a death sentence for most people, doctors often went to heroic measures to save their patients, especially in the operating room.

Resting, Collapsing, Removing

One surgical procedure was called pneumothorax—a scientific name for the collapsing of a lung. Many doctors believed that rest was vital for the tuberculosis patient; yet while patients dozed in chairs or slept in their beds, the part of their bodies that most needed rest—their lungs—continued to work. Pneumothorax was based on the idea that if a diseased lung could rest for a period of time, it might become healthier. Some doctors even claimed that the procedure could result in a cure, since collapsing a lung would deprive the bacilli of oxygen, and they would die.

The procedure was first done in Italy in the late 1800s but became very common in the United States by the 1920s and 1930s. By 1937 it was estimated that between 50 and 80 percent of patients at the larger U.S. sanatoriums were undergoing the procedure. The surgeon would use a needle to inject a quantity of air into the chest cavity, between the affected lung and ribs. Since the lungs are flexible and soft, they can easily adapt to a smaller environment. When surgeons collapsed a lung, they were actually collapsing the space around it so that the lung could not expand to its regular size. As a result, the lung's capacity would significantly decrease.

Pneumothorax was considered a minor operation—usually performed at a patient's bedside, often without anesthetic. A more radical form of surgery included the removal of a number of ribs—sometimes as many as nine. Sometimes this was done to create an even greater space for an air cushion. In other instances, it allowed the chest wall to simply collapse on itself, making less space for the diseased lung to expand. Though a patient was anesthetized for rib removal, it was still a painful operation and was attempted only on a seriously ill patient.

Something from the Soil

At the same time that doctors were experimenting with surgical techniques, researchers were working on medicines that might be effective in killing the tubercle bacillus. For a short time in 1928, scientists believed that the antibiotic penicillin might be effective in treating tuberculosis. Penicillin, a natural substance that comes from

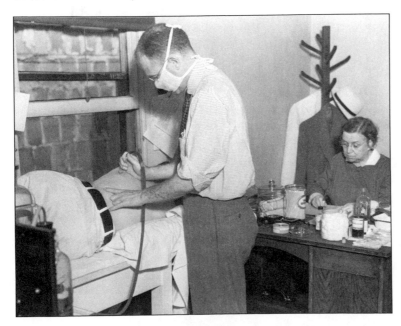

A doctor gives a patient pneumothorax treatment, which collapses a lung in order to let it rest.

bread mold, was found to kill certain bacteria that it came into contact with.

But while penicillin was highly effective against some bacteria, such as those that cause pneumonia and some sexually transmitted diseases, it had no effect on the tubercle bacillus. Even so, the discovery invigorated other scientists and gave them a reason to look for other naturally occurring antibiotics.

In 1943, a breakthrough was made in the Rutgers University research laboratories in New Jersey. Dr. Selman Waksman, an immigrant from the Ukraine, was extremely interested in the tiny organisms that inhabit the soil. A local farmer told Waksman that he had a chicken that had become ill after pecking in the soft dirt around the farm. Wondering if the soil contained something that would endanger his whole flock, the farmer asked Waksman for help.

After examining the soil and the microorganisms it held, Waksman and his assistant, Albert Schatz, found a mold that was similar in some ways to penicillin. Like penicillin, this mold generated a substance that killed certain bacteria—including the TB germ. This substance, known as streptomycin, would change the entire method by which tuberculosis was treated around the world.

"And—Incredibly—I Did Feel Strong Enough"

By 1944 streptomycin was being tested in clinical trials on humans, especially those for whom surgery and sanatorium stays had failed. The results were almost miraculous: People who had been near death steadily improved. One young man, who had been told by staff at his sanatorium not to leave his room, since his appearance was bad for morale, recalled how amazed he was when after several dosages of the new medicine, he felt so much better than he had in years:

> "[The doctor] hummed and haaed for awhile," he wrote in his diary, "then informed me that well, there was no reason,

if I felt strong enough, why I shouldn't spend some time in the lounge or in the library. Even go for a short walk. And—incredibly—I did feel strong enough."[73]

Soon, instead of growing cultures of the drug in their laboratory for use on certain patients, Waksman and his associates made arrangements for the drug to be mass-produced by drug companies in large fifteen-thousand-gallon drums. Doctors all over the world were clamoring for supplies of the new medicine.

Triple Therapy

But while streptomycin was effective against the TB bacillus much of the time, the drug could produce unpleasant side effects in some patients, such as fatigue, muscle aches, fevers, and a red, itchy rash. Besides causing side effects, streptomycin was apparently unable to cure some strains of TB.

Interestingly, at almost the same time that Waksman and his associates were working on that drug, a Danish scientist had been exploring the bacteria-killing abilities of another substance known as para-aminosalicylic acid (PAS), which is related to aspirin. When PAS was found to inhibit the growth of the TB bacillus, doctors began using it along with streptomycin—with excellent results. And a third drug, isoniazid, was introduced in 1952. It was found to be effective when combined with PAS and streptomycin.

After so many years of failure by researchers looking for a cure, three workable medicines were developed within a decade of one another. Known as the "triple therapy," these drugs taken together effectively wiped out the germ that had caused so much death and destruction over the centuries.

Gone

In a short time, there were clear signs that the era of the sanatorium and pneumothorax surgery had come to an abrupt halt. Saranac Lake and other sanatoriums closed their doors, their patients having taken their medicine and returned home. The anti-tuberculosis leagues dissipated, after having been so active only months before in promoting healthy living and an end to the germ-infested tenements. With little to fear from tuberculosis, their supporters lost interest. Selman Waksman, who was later honored with the Nobel Prize for his discovery of streptomycin, noted in 1964—twenty years after his achievement—that "a disease that less than two decades ago was regarded as the greatest threat to the health and life of man . . . has been reduced to the tenth position or even farther back, among the killers of human beings."[74]

New antibiotics were found that were more powerful against the TB germ as well as less likely to cause side effects. Doctors who had previously specialized in tuberculosis found that their years of experience were, for all

Dr. Selman Waksman, who discovered streptomycin, a mold similar to penicillin, that kills TB germs.

intents and purposes, useless. "By degrees," writes one doctor, "for the ordinary man and woman on the street, tuberculosis began to fade from consciousness."[75] No one was coughing up blood; no one was dying from TB. Or at least, that appeared to be the case.

"TB Was Almost a Joke"

Doctors were aware that the disease had not disappeared completely. Around the world, especially in developing nations, TB was still a problem in some places. Even in the United States, tuberculosis still lived—especially in the poorest neighborhoods of big cities, on Native American reservations, and in other pockets of extreme poverty.

But no one could argue with numbers, and they indicated that tuberculosis—especially in the United States—had become rare. Thanks to the new, more powerful drugs that had been developed, TB would soon be a thing of the past, like cholera and smallpox.

That is why, when a Princeton University graduate student named Walter Moberg got sick in 1985, doctors were amazed. Moberg had been doing volunteer work with the homeless in Portland, Oregon, when he developed a bad cough and sought medical help. "When [the doctors] finally diagnosed it," recalls Moberg, "they seemed amused. One doctor told me a joke. 'TB or not TB: that is the congestion. Consumption be done about it? Of cough, of cough. But it takes a lung, lung time.' TB was almost a joke."[76]

"I Felt So Immune"

Moberg's case of tuberculosis was startling—both to him and to his doctors—given the current status of the disease. However, Moberg was not as rare a case as public health officials believed. In fact, in New York City the number of cases—which had been decreasing since the 1950s—had begun climbing in 1978.

By 1989, Jack Adler, the medical director of the New York Bureau of Tuberculosis, reported that the year's rise

A New York Police Officer Gets TB

Although many of the new TB cases are found among immigrant or homeless urban populations, some people never considered themselves at risk of catching the disease. One of these people, a New York City police officer who has MDR tuberculosis, is profiled in Geraldine Baum's article, "An Ill Wind in New York," from the Los Angeles Times.

Tuberculosis has turned up with such force in Gustavo Linares' body that it has gnawed tiny holes through his lungs, reduced him to 115 pounds and left the once-strapping New York City policeman isolated in a hospital room with a mask over his face.

An ex-Marine, Linares may never be well enough to move back to Queens with his wife and 11-year-old daughter. He may never regain hearing lost as a side effect from his medicine. And he may never be cured. He is 36 years old and believes he caught the disease one winter while corralling the homeless into shelters.

"Too bad I didn't listen," he says, his voice lost in a clot of fluid. "I didn't always take the medicine like they told me. I would feel better in a few weeks, then stop. . . . "

Linares pauses mid-sentence to turn his face toward the window, as if to make room for the air he hopes will constitute his next breath. On the seventh floor of Bellevue Hospital, a behemoth public institution, Linares has a rare private room and a dramatic view of the East River. Most days, he is flopped on the bed, alternately watching television and helicopters floating across the river, carting executives to the Big City.

"I know I've done a lot of things wrong," he says, referring to his habit of stopping and starting his pills, which left him resistant to first-line drugs. "I'm wasting away like they used to . . . in the old days."

in case numbers "represents a 9.8 percent increase over 1988's and a 68 percent increase over 1980's. The 1989 case rate is the highest in two decades."[77] By 1995, health officials were calling New York's skyrocketing TB rate a full-blown emergency.

And while most of those infected were immigrants living in poorer neighborhoods, some perplexing cases were found among rural, middle-class families. In North

Tarrytown, an upper-middle-class town north of New York, newborn twins were suffering from a bad cold that would not go away. Their parents—both lawyers—and another brother soon developed the illness, and doctors diagnosed it as tuberculosis.

The family, like the doctors, was stunned at the news. No one seriously considered that TB was a risk in such a community. "I felt so immune," said the mother of the twins. "We live in this tiny town in Westchester, in the middle of the forest."[78]

What Went Wrong?

The return of tuberculosis puzzled many experts. What had happened, they wondered, to allow a supposedly "tamed" germ to return? As they eventually learned, there were many reasons.

One was cockiness, plain and simple. Because tuberculosis had become invisible in developed nations— wiped out from all but the most impoverished communities—the public virtually forgot about it. In the United States, anti-tuberculosis programs no longer received much community support after 1960.

The situation in the medical community was not much better. The best and the brightest of the new medical researchers were more interested in genetics, cancer, or the new viruses that were showing up around the world than they were in tuberculosis. Funding for tuberculosis research was slashed and state and local programs often died out, the money allotted to them routed elsewhere. Hospital wards that had reserved beds for tuberculosis patients used the space for other things. Clinics that had been working diligently with immigrants and lower-income people to educate them about the disease and its cure no longer concentrated on TB. Public health officials readily admit that they were far too smug about having stamped out tuberculosis before they actually had. "It is an embarrassment to my profession," says a researcher today.[79]

"I Got No Stomach for That"

Experts agree that a big reason for the increase in the spread of tuberculosis has been the ballooning populations of homeless people since the mid-1980s—a result of social service cutbacks. Because of overcrowded shelters and the poor hygiene practices of some shelter residents, contagious diseases are easily passed from one person to another. In this excerpt from a personal interview with the author, a homeless immigrant from Guatemala talks about life in some of the shelters he has lived in over the past several years.

"Me, I prefer living by myself, living alone," he says, lighting the stump of a cigarette he has pulled from the pocket of his jeans.

"I hate living with the kind of people who are there. That sounds funny, I know. I'm one of the people, right? But it's true. Some of them have never taken a bath, they've never been told about keeping their hands clean. They don't change underwear.

"And they got no excuses, because there's some group that donates stuff for the shelter where we eat. A church group, I think. They have little bundles they give the men—has a stick of deodorant, a new pair of shorts [underwear], a toothbrush. But some of these guys, they just take the bundle and throw it. They don't care.

"See, I hate even going a day without brushing my teeth. I don't feel clean unless I do that. But that's upbringing, am I right? That's your mother and your father teaching you as you grow up, how to take care of yourself.

"Maybe these guys had no parents like I had back home. I shouldn't pass judgment, but I do. I know I do. I should be more tolerant. But I hate it . . . guys blowing their noses in their hand, doing whatever they want. That stuff makes me sick inside, you know? I got a weak stomach. Like I had a bed one night, and there was junk all over the pillow. I told the lady, give me another pillowcase, okay? So's I can cover up both ends, because there's snot or something all over it, and I can't fall asleep putting my head on that.

"She says she only got one [pillow]case to a customer, so I left. I got no stomach for that. That's just the way I am."

Public Health Malpractice

But it was not just the medical community that was at fault. Some blame must be laid at the feet of politicians and those who elected them. Social conditions worsened in the 1980s, when the Reagan and Bush administrations discontinued or cut funding for many programs dealing with health services and housing for the poorest Americans. As a result, a huge increase in homelessness over the past twenty years has forced people into dirty, crowded conditions—into shelters that, because of staff shortages, are not cleaned adequately. In addition, say experts, the poor (whether homeless or not) are far less likely to eat a healthy diet, get fresh air, or refrain from unhealthy lifestyles that increase the risk of catching tuberculosis.

Warnings along the way were largely ignored. In 1989 when the Centers for Disease Control and Prevention created a plan to tackle the resurging tuberculosis problem, it was met with apathy by both the U.S. Senate and White House. And when the plan was resurrected four years later—at a much higher price, because of the continued spread of TB—the Clinton administration

President Bill Clinton, whose administration pared away 75 percent of a proposed plan to combat the resurgence of TB.

pared away 75 percent of the amount allocated to the plan before routing it to Congress. One California representative denied that only one political party was to blame for the lack of support. "If there were such a thing as public health malpractice," he said, "all three administrations [Reagan, Bush, and Clinton] would be guilty."[80]

MDR—The Superbug

No sooner had TB resurfaced than the medical community was struck with an even more frightening reality. Many of the new tuberculosis cases did not respond to the modern equivalent of the triple therapy. These drugs, which had once worked so well against every case of tuberculosis, often did nothing to control a patient's symptoms.

Thus, people were not only catching TB but also dying from it. "It was," explains one Chicago physician, "as if we'd time-traveled back to the 1920s or something. We'd try a few more things, and if they didn't work, we just scratched our heads and said we were sorry—we didn't have much of anything that could help. It was like being back in the pre–antibiotic age again, with no weapons."[81]

Cases that did not respond to any of the triple therapy medications became known as multi-drug-resistant (MDR). Of course, doctors had other drugs to try; in the years after the triple therapy, other antibiotics had been developed that could sometimes be effective against tuberculosis. But these "second-line" drugs, as they are known, have a downside: They are either less powerful or result in unpleasant side effects for the patient.

Doctors have no way of telling whether a patient has MDR tuberculosis before they prescribe medication. The process begins with the frontline drugs— the triple therapy. A patient who does not respond is then moved to the second-line medications. Unfortunately, the cure rate between those with regular tuberculosis and MDR TB is staggering: Ninety-six percent of those with regular TB are cured with the frontline drugs. The MDR patients who must rely on second-line drugs get well only about 50 percent of the time.

"A Word of Four Letters"

Scientists know that there are several reasons for the drug-resistant strains of tuberculosis that have appeared. But few disagree with the most important reason. "I can give it to you in a word of four letters," says one New York researcher: "AIDS."[82]

A healthy person's immune system provides natural resistance to diseases such as tuberculosis. The bacteria usually lie dormant in the system, often for the remainder of the person's life, without ever developing into tuberculosis. Doctors say that only one out of ten people who are infected ever develop that disease.

But AIDS destroys the immune system, leaving the body an easy target. The AIDS patient has a one out of ten chance of developing TB—not in a lifetime, but within a year of being infected. And TB infection for an AIDS patient is far more serious than it would be in someone without a weakened immune system.

Researchers have also learned that the tuberculosis germ and the AIDS virus seem to work together, as one doctor says, "in a synergy of terror never seen before in medical history."[83] Under normal conditions, a person can live for years with AIDS or tuberculosis alone. However, together each speeds up the rate of the other; the combination can make a person deathly ill very quickly. Worse, a patient with both AIDS and TB often develops a strain of tuberculosis that is drug-resistant. That explains why TB in an AIDS patient is so often fatal—more than 80 percent of the time.

Only Part of the Cause

AIDS has enabled the tubercle bacillus to mutate to more drug-resistant forms. But AIDS is certainly not the only reason for what doctors often refer to as the TB superbugs. Virulent strains of tuberculosis that are drug-resistant have developed because of patients not taking their full course of medicine.

People diagnosed with TB are put on a strict regimen of ten to sixteen pills every day, for six to twelve months.

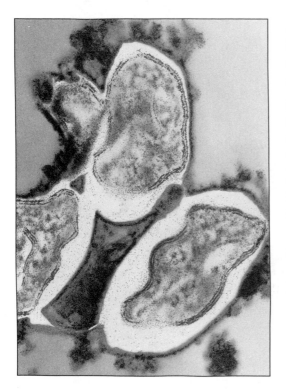

*Drug-resistant TB
bacteria (pictured)
cannot be killed by the
frontline drugs that
doctors normally use to
treat tuberculosis.*

At the end of that time, their disease is almost always gone. If a person does not finish the medicine or uses it only sporadically, an extremely dangerous situation can arise. For while many of the tuberculosis germs could be wiped out with only a partial regimen of drugs, a few more hardy ones will be left. If allowed to remain in the body, they breed, creating a strain that is drug-resistant.

"We've been seeing this same phenomenon with penicillin for years," says one clinic nurse. "We'll see a baby with an ear infection, and the doctor sends the parents home with two weeks' worth of medicine. But the baby feels better after a couple of days—and besides, it's often hard to give medication to a baby anyway—so the rest of the medicine just gets thrown away. But the next ear infection, maybe that medicine isn't going to do much good. It's survival of the fittest—and we're letting the tough germs live on."[84]

Discouraging Statistics

Tuberculosis drugs can produce positive results very quickly, just as penicillin can on a baby's ear infection. TB patients taking these drugs may find that their fever disappears, or that their cough is less severe. And because they feel better, they are less likely to make taking medicine a priority.

The poor are the most likely to discontinue medication, especially if they are living in homeless shelters. "For the homeless," says one researcher, "who scrounge daily for food and shelter, the need to take medicine after symptoms have vanished is a relatively minor concern."[85]

It is little wonder then, that so many of the homeless TB patients return to clinics months after they were first diagnosed—and learn that their disease is back in a more dangerous form. Some estimate that one-third of the TB cases among homeless populations in New York and Chicago are drug-resistant.

Breathing as a Risk

The skyrocketing numbers of MDR tuberculosis cases frighten health care workers, who know such strains are extremely contagious. "It's not like AIDS," says one nurse, "where you can really cut down your risk if you eliminate the dangerous behaviors. If you practice safe sex, if you don't share needles, things like that—it's pretty hard to get it. But TB is everywhere—really, it's everywhere."[86] Leading tuberculosis researcher Barry Bloom agrees. "The major risk factor for acquiring tuberculosis," he notes, "is breathing."[87]

Examples abound that prove how easily TB is spread. Debi French, the California teen who barely survived a bout with MDR tuberculosis, is thought to have caught it merely from attending school with an infected student whom she never even met. Five school bus drivers with TB in Long Island, New York, infected forty-one young students in 1994. The threat of catching TB, whether you are rich or poor, young or old, is all too real. "Tuberculosis can be spread by one cough," writes TB expert Paul Farmer. "It can be transported from one country to another in a single plane ride."[88]

With news so dire, the question that arises is simple: What can be done? With one-third of the world's population carrying the bacteria in their lungs, and more than 1 billion new cases—and 70 million deaths—predicted by 2020, is there any way of stopping tuberculosis?

CHAPTER 6

Not Only a Medical Problem

The new battle against tuberculosis is being fought on many fronts. Obviously, medical research will play a very important role. No new drugs for tuberculosis have been developed since the late 1960s. Research facilities around the world are searching for more powerful drugs to take the place of those that are now ineffective against MDR tuberculosis.

A Deeper Look at the Tubercle Bacillus

One positive development is that some of medicine's most talented researchers are now becoming involved in tuberculosis research. Among those are DNA specialists, who believe that the best strategy in finding a real cure is to look at the disease not as a collection of symptoms, but far deeper—on the genetic level.

After all, they say, bacteria are living things, just as plants and animals are. The bacteria tubercle bacillus, like all other living things, has a genetic code that determines all its characteristics. Using a host of new tools, scientists are trying to understand which genes within the bacillus make it so deadly. Specific information like this, say experts, would be helpful in finding a medicine that would work not just on most patients, but on all patients—even those who have MDR tuberculosis.

Such work has already had promising results by prompting a closer look at a drug that has been used against TB since the 1950s. Isoniazid, the third medication in what was known as the triple therapy, was prescribed routinely, yet doctors were never sure why it worked. But researchers at Albert Einstein College of Medicine in New York recently used their high-tech genetic tools to look at the interaction between the drug and the TB bacillus—and they were amazed at what they found.

"We Have a Drug!"

Isoniazid actually blocks the activity of one of the tuberculosis genes. This gene contains a code that allows the TB germ to create long chains of fatty acids, which are used as a wall. This fatty acid chain keeps the bacillus

A scientist prepares slides for gene mapping, a process that allows the genetic code of TB germs to be studied.

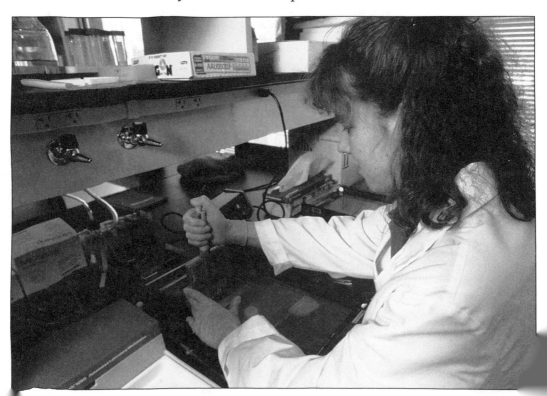

from being invaded by the body's natural disease fighters, as well as by many medicines. But isoniazid interferes with that gene, stopping the building of the fatty acid walls and allowing other medications to invade the bacteria.

"The researchers sat down," explains Stephen Hall, who spent time observing the group's work, "rearranged a few atoms, and designed a new chemical that they thought would block this key [gene] even better than isoniazid." They tinkered around further and came up with a substance that, in a test tube, seems to be ruthless at knocking out the TB germ. The researchers were euphoric, says Hall. He remembers one shout, "We have a drug!"[89]

Needing to Shorten the Wait

Many more experiments must be completed to establish how safe the substance is and to determine any long-range problems or side effects. That will take years; even so, researchers are encouraged by what they see as a promising new way to approach the disease.

In the meantime, they are applying some of the same ideas to solving another problem that doctors who treat TB patients face—that of not knowing early enough whether a patient has a standard strain of tuberculosis or a drug-resistant strain. Because the TB bacillus is an extremely slow-growing organism, doctors need to see it multiply and grow in a culture before they know what will work against it. (Scientists can learn far more about bacteria by observing them in large groups.) Such waiting, says researcher Bill Jacobs, can waste valuable time—sometimes time that a patient does not have:

> You culture a patient's strain [sputum with bacteria in it] and then it takes five weeks to grow it up and another five weeks to test its susceptibility to drugs. But within a month, the patient comes back to the hospital. He's doing worse. You suspect drug-resistant TB, so you start him on two other drugs. Another month later, he's dead. Two weeks

after that, you find out he was infected with a particular kind of multidrug-resistant TB—and if you had known which drugs he was resistant to and which ones he was still sensitive to, you could have put the patient on a very different set of drugs."[90]

Help from Fireflies

But the genetic technology used in learning about isoniazid has been helpful with this problem, too. Jacobs and fellow researchers have studied tiny viruses, known as "phage," that are naturally found in dirt. Phage often infect various bacteria—including the TB bacillus.

A New Screening Test Is Needed

In its February 2000 article, "TB Easier to Transmit than Standard Test Reveals," USA Today Magazine raises the worrisome question about the validity of the most widely used screening test for tuberculosis.

The standard test for gauging whether a tuberculosis patient is infectious misses half the people capable of transmitting the disease, a Stanford University Medical Center study found. After using DNA fingerprinting to track TB spread in San Francisco, the researchers concluded that patients classified as non-infectious by the test nevertheless gave rise to one-sixth of new cases. "Only half of TB patients are detected by this test, yet the other half are still infectious and continue to propagate this epidemic," notes Marcel Behr, lead author of the study.

For diagnosing tuberculosis and determining the severity of a patient's illness, TB control programs worldwide rely on a test called the acid-fast bacilli (AFB) smear. In this fast, cheap, and simple method, a sample of sputum (better known as phlegm) is inspected under a light microscope for the presence of tuberculosis bacteria. Positive results mean the patient should immediately be placed in isolation in a hospital, because every cough could launch enough bacteria to infect many other people. Negative results have generally been interpreted to mean that the patient is non-infectious and requires no special precautions.

However, theoretical and experimental results have cast doubt on the ability of this workhorse test to detect infectious patients, maintains Peter Small, assistant professor of medicine. Although as few as five TB bacteria bedding down in the lungs can start a new infection, a sample must contain 5,000–10,000 bacteria per milliliter to reach the test's threshold of detection. . . .

"For any other disease, we wouldn't tolerate a diagnostic test that only picks up half the cases," Behr emphasizes.

The next step the scientists took was to isolate a firefly's gene—the one that produces the firefly's glow—and insert it into one of the phage. When that is done, explains Hall, "the gene turns on—and the chemical glows—when the phage multiply, and the phage multiply only when their hosts, [the TB bacteria] are themselves alive and kicking."[91]

From that step, the researchers were able to take another. The glow-in-the-dark viruses allow a rapid test that shows which drugs will work for a patient and which will not. Taking a series of test tubes of bacteria from a patient, they add the glowing phage, which quickly infect the bacteria. Then they add a different TB drug to each test tube. The bacteria that is killed by a drug will not glow, while the drug-resistant germs will continue to do so. This test will be expensive to produce, but once available, it will make doctors' jobs much easier.

More than New Drugs

Combating TB in the twenty-first century will entail more than creating new medicines and diagnostic tests in laboratories. A large amount of effort needs to be spent educating people about the proper way of caring for themselves if they are diagnosed with tuberculosis. Knowing how to minimize the risk to others by proper hygiene is important. And understanding how crucial it is to take all medication, no matter how well a patient feels, is critical.

Many challenges are involved in educating an at-risk population. In the United States, for example, many of those with TB are recent immigrants. Health care workers encounter a number of barriers when dealing with them. Often, the barrier is one of language; for example, Spanish-speaking patients who are unable to understand detailed instructions from an English-speaking doctor are probably headed for problems, say experts. Having on staff at clinics and hospitals at least one person who can communicate with patients in their own language is necessary.

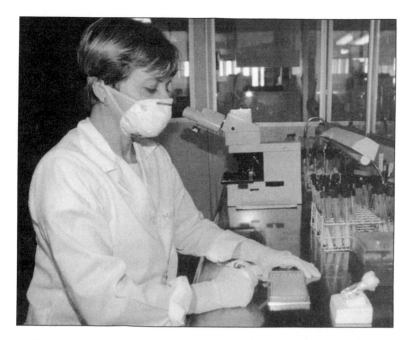

A researcher tests different strains of tuberculosis.

Sometimes other barriers may prevent people from going to a clinic in the first place—even when they suspect that they are seriously ill. The barrier in this case may be one of shame or social embarrassment, says one Minneapolis doctor who treats many tuberculosis patients. "In the Somali community," he says, "somebody who is affected by tuberculosis is seen as someone who is cursed."[92]

Rather than be scorned by neighbors, a sick Somali may choose to disguise the fact that he or she is seriously ill for as long as possible. Not only is this person endangering himself or herself by not treating the illness, he or she is putting family and friends in danger by exposing them to tuberculosis.

Thinking Globally

If there is one lesson to be learned since the 1950s, when tuberculosis was thought to be conquered, it is that the energy of combating the disease must not end at a nation's borders. As long as people anywhere in the world are infected with TB, it will present a danger to everyone.

The Death of Annette Jean

Tuberculosis is an epidemic in many countries around the world, including Haiti. In his book, Infections and Inequalities: The Modern Plagues, *medical expert Paul Farmer describes the death of a young woman brought to his clinic—too late.*

Early on the morning of her death, Annette Jean was feeling well enough to fetch a heavy bucket of water from a spring not far from her family's hut. In the weeks prior to that day, she had been complaining of a "cold." It was not serious, she thought, although night sweats and a loss of appetite were beginning to trouble her. Annette's brothers later recalled that she was cheerful, "normal," that morning. She made everyone coffee and helped her mother load up the donkey for market. It was an overcast day in October of 1994, and Haiti's rainy season was drawing to a close.

Shortly after Annette's brothers left for their garden, the young woman abruptly began coughing up blood. A young cousin, watching from across the yard, saw her throw off a bright red arc and then collapse on the dirt floor of the tiny house. The child ran for Annette's three brothers, who tried in vain to rouse her; the young woman could do no more than gurgle in response to their panicked cries. The brothers then hastily confected a stretcher from sheets and saplings. It would take them more than an hour, carrying their inert sister, to reach the nearest clinic. . . .

Halfway there, it began to rain. The steep path became slippery, further impeding progress. Two-thirds of the way there, Annette coughed up clots of darker blood and then stopped gurgling. By the time they reached the clinic, it was raining heavily. The larger clots refused to melt, hardening on her soaked shirt, and Annette was motionless in a puddle of diluted blood. She was not yet twenty years old.

That has been the message of the World Health Organization (WHO), which since 1948 has been the United Nation's authority on public health issues around the world. According to WHO, 90 percent of TB cases are occurring in developing nations or those that are in chaos because of political reorganization, such as Russia or the Czech Republic. In these nations, consistent health care is often difficult to attain even for people with money or position; for the poor it is usually nonexistent.

For the rest of the world to feel comfortable curing only the cases in their own country is foolish, say WHO workers. Because of the need for international cooperation, organizations such as the International Red Cross, Doctors Without Borders, and the Medical Emergency Relief Network need to get involved—and soon. "If we want to control TB," proclaims one health official, "we need to go to the countries where TB is."[93]

A Daunting Task in Russia

But that is not an easy task. In 1997 WHO first published a list of the TB "hot spots"—those places where the disease not only is flourishing but has mutated to MDR status at an alarming rate. Any nation in which 5 percent or more of the tuberculosis population is resistant to at least two frontline drugs was listed as a hot spot. In 1997 eight nations fit this description; the list was updated in 1999 to one hundred nations, and some believe the list will grow by 2005.

The roadblocks encountered in fighting TB are even more daunting in these hot spots. Not enough doctors and clinics are available to adequately serve the numbers of sick people who seek help. And most clinics do not have the resources to battle tuberculosis without help.

Russia is a good example of a country where tuberculosis is out of control, especially in the prison system's holding centers. These are filthy and overcrowded, and they reek of spoiled food and unwashed bodies. Prisoners there wait for a court date for months, and sometimes years, in areas that are so overcrowded that prisoners must sleep in shifts. The estimate in 2000 was that more than 10 percent of the prisoners in the country (about 110,000 people) have active tuberculosis. In some prisons, more than 90 percent of those with tuberculosis have MDR TB.

A Deadly Problem

It is not that Russian doctors do not know how to treat
TB; they simply do not have the resources. For example,
one small prison has nine hundred men who need treatment for tuberculosis, yet the prison's budget for medication and supplies is about the equivalent of two
thousand American dollars. Therefore, the prison can
only afford to purchase a supply of some frontline drugs.
Second-line drugs are much more expensive—as well as
harder to get in Russia.

Frontline drugs are not helping many of the prisoners
with MDR TB. And that is bad news for them and for the
villages and towns where they come from. For when
these prisoners are released back into the general population when their sentences have been served, they will
be carrying a lethally dangerous, highly contagious illness.

This, say scientists, is how an epidemic gains momen-
tum. Thousands of prisoners with a disease that does not
respond to drugs each infect an average of anywhere
between fifteen and twenty other people. And those
people, in turn, will become sick and will infect others.
Public health official Alex Goldfarb shakes his head at
the almost automatic infection rate of Russian prisoners.
"It is a pump," he says. "Practically everyone who goes
there gets TB, and every year 300,000 prisoners leave."[94]

Even worse, in an effort to save money and relieve the
overcrowding in their prisons, the Russian justice department at the end of the millennium declared a prison
amnesty. "That means," writes one expert, "that nearly
90,000 newly released prisoners will be on Russian streets
this summer, the height of tourist season. No fewer than
a third will have the drug-resistant strain of TB."[95]

"I Felt Ashamed"

Similar stories abound in many countries throughout
the world: Peru, El Salvador, Laos, Haiti, Somalia, the
Ivory Coast. For a variety of reasons, seriously ill people
are getting scanty treatment—or no treatment at all. Kris

Johnson is a twenty-one-year-old nursing student who recently went to El Salvador as part of an educational project. Helping in several rural clinics, she was appalled at what she considers needless deaths:

> I honestly said to myself, "This is completely unacceptable." After all, this is the 21st century—people are not supposed to be dying like this. We have medicines that can cure tuberculosis and other things. But in just the seven weeks I was there I saw—I personally watched—as maybe thirty people died.
>
> For me, any death is hard, no matter if the person dies of old age or because of an accident or a heart attack. And I think I was actually more prepared for cases of AIDS, cancer, things that we don't have real cures for yet. But something like TB? It's almost like watching people starving—it isn't supposed to happen these days. I don't know—I felt ashamed that we're not doing more.[96]

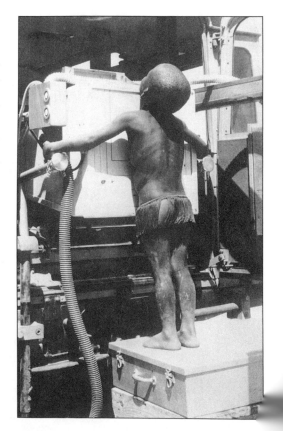

An African boy holds on to an X-ray machine in order to be examined for tuberculosis.

Tackling Two Major Problems

Addressing the problem of tuberculosis around the world involves activity on various levels, not the least of which is economic. The cost for tuberculosis drugs is high. Even for combating regular TB, the cost for a single patient can run as high as $2,000. But the second-line medications that patients with MDR tuberculosis need run far more—at $19,000.

Since 1999, the World Health Organization has been formulating a strategy that they believe could revolutionize TB treatment all over the world. Their aim was to eliminate the two biggest problems in fighting tuberculosis: a lack of medicine in many areas and the inability of doctors to see that patients take their medicine correctly.

To achieve this aim, they worked for a global drug facility—a sort of clearinghouse for all TB medications, both frontline and those for MDR TB. WHO would work with pharmaceutical manufacturers around the world to attempt to have a ready supply of the drugs for any nation that needed them, and at a reasonable cost. No nation, no matter how poor, would be left out.

In the summer of 2001, WHO announced that it had finally made a significant breakthrough in their efforts: not only would both frontline and second-line drugs be available, but also the price would be significantly reduced for nations that could not afford them. Some nations, it was reported, would be able to save almost 94 percent on their current spending for second-line drugs.

Dr. Gro Harlem Brundtland, the director-general of WHO, was pleased with the development, for it showed that the nations of the world were finally understanding the necessity of working together against tuberculosis. "International approaches to reducing TB drug prices," she noted, "show that the international TB partnership can make a significant difference to people suffering from multi-drug-resistant TB."[97]

A Second Problem

Health officials call the announcement a good start; however, they are aware that a ready supply of medicine will be a solution to only one obstacle in the international TB battle. The second obstacle is in making sure that patients take their regimen of medications. That is a problem that has been frustrating health workers around the world.

One reason patients discontinue their medication is because they feel better, and it is difficult to remember to take medicine unless they feel sick—especially the ten to sixteen pills they are supposed to take each day for a year. But those who have MDR tuberculosis commonly stop their medication for another reason: side effects.

The second-line drugs—sixteen pills each day—are far more toxic to the system than the frontline drugs, and may cause nausea, severe abdominal cramping, headaches, fatigue, nosebleeds, and short-term memory loss. Some patients lose their hearing. Such unpleasant side effects, combined with the longer drug regimen for MDR TB (two years), make it easy to understand why these patients are often erratic in taking their medicine.

DOT

The plan for which WHO has had high hopes since it was first implemented in 1993 is known as DOT, for Directly Observed Treatment. The idea is that people must take their medication in the presence of a doctor or clinic worker, to prevent them from discontinuing it too soon. WHO hopes that by making DOT a part of the low-cost drug clearinghouse, it will be implemented in a disciplined way.

Without question, such observed treatment can significantly reduce the number of deaths from tuberculosis. Some nations, such as China and Peru, have reported that their cure rates in areas where DOT is used have risen by 50 percent. In addition, the number of drug-resistant cases in those same areas has been reduced. However, by 1999 it was clear that while 120 countries around the world had adopted the DOT program, only 23 percent of the tuberculosis patients were being treated.

Troubling Reactions

Various factors have impeded the DOT program in certain countries. Some areas have met with resistance from patients who find it difficult to travel from remote rural areas to clinics each day to take medicine. Some patients are also wary of being known as TB patients; they worry about participating in any program in which their health status will be known.

Sometimes, too, the problem is not as much with patients as with the governments themselves. For instance, some nations have balked at the cost of supervising patients, as well as the idea of an outside agency (WHO) monitoring the health of their citizens. Russian doctors have complained that they are offended by the idea that they need the DOT system. To use it, they say, would be akin to admitting they are unable to handle their own problems. "It's good for places like Africa and Southeast Asia," says one Russian doctor. "But it doesn't really apply to Russia."[98]

The Years Ahead

But WHO directors are optimistic. They believe that ultimately the program will work, especially in light of the low-cost drugs soon to be available to nations that will make a commitment to eradicating TB. They hope that physicians throughout the world will act quickly, taking advantage of the resources now available to them and to their patients. In addition, they look forward to exciting new technologies—more powerful drugs or, even better, an effective vaccine that could immunize the entire world.

However, some experts are more guarded in their speculation. They have real concerns whether nations can put aside political or social agendas long enough to deal with this disease. They point out, quite accurately, that tuberculosis is not "coming back," for it never left in the first place. It merely became invisible by retreating to the poorest communities around the world. "The neglect of tuberculosis as a major public health priority over the past two decades is simply extraordinary," wrote one expert in 1991. "Perhaps the most important contributor to this state of ignorance was the greatly reduced . . . importance of tuberculosis in the wealthy nations."[99]

Medical researchers and physicians are waging war against the oldest, most prolific killer in the world. The hope is that the closely intertwined world population, as well as the highly contagious nature of tuberculosis, will serve as reminders that all nations must be involved. Whether people can win the war will be determined

partly by exciting medical breakthroughs. Just as crucial, however, will be making sure that these breakthroughs—whether new medicines, vaccines, or diagnostic tools—are available to everyone. Unless that happens, everyone will lose.

A TB patient in a refugee hospital in Somalia.

NOTES

Introduction: The Disease That Survived Its Own Death

1. *Time*, "TB—and Hope," March 3, 1952, p. 42.
2. *Time*, "TB—and Hope," p. 42.
3. Quoted in Mark Caldwell, *The Last Crusade: The War on Consumption, 1862–1954*. New York: Atheneum, 1998.
4. Quoted in Sheila M. Rothman, *Living in the Shadow of Death: Tuberculosis and the Social Experience of Illness in American History*. New York: Basic Books, 1994, p. 249.
5. Quoted in Leslie Roberts, "The Comeback Plague," *U.S. News & World Report*, March 27, 2000, p. 50.
6. Quoted in Roberts, "The Comeback Plague," p. 50.

Chapter 1: The White Plague

7. Thomas Dormandy, *The White Death: A History of Tuberculosis*. New York: New York University Press, 1999, p. 2.
8. Quoted in Dormandy, *The White Death*, pp. 2–3.
9. Quoted in René and Jean Dubos, *The White Plague: Tuberculosis, Man, and Society*. 1952. Reprint, New Brunswick, NJ: Rutgers University Press, 1987, p. 8.
10. Quoted in Dubos, *The White Plague*, p. 9.
11. Quoted in Rothman, *Living in the Shadow of Death*, p. 14.
12. Caldwell, *The Last Crusade*, p. 17.
13. Katherine Ott, *Fevered Lives: Tuberculosis in American Culture Since 1870*. Cambridge: Harvard University Press, 1996, p. 13.
14. Quoted in Dormandy, *The White Death*, pp. 93–94.

15. Dubos, *The White Plague*, p. 18.
16. Quoted in Ken Chowder, "How TB Survived Its Own Death to Confront Us Again," *Smithsonian*, November 1992, p. 180.
17. Dormandy, *The White Death*, p. 91.
18. Quoted in Dormandy, *The White Death*, p. 91.
19. Dubos, *The White Plague*, pp. 65–66.
20. Quoted in Dormandy, *The White Death*, p. 141.
21. John Bessner Huber, *Consumption: Its Relation to Man and His Civilization, Its Prevention and Cure.* Philadelphia: J. B. Lippincott, 1906, p. 103.
22. Dormandy, *The White Death*, p. 44.
23. Ott, *Fevered Lives*, p. 50.
24. Quoted in Dormandy, *The White Death*, p. 46.
25. Dormandy, *The White Death*, p. 48.

Chapter 2: Fighting Tuberculosis

26. Quoted in Dubos, *The White Plague*, p. 85.
27. Quoted in Dormandy, *The White Death*, p. 34.
28. Dormandy, *The White Death*, p. 56.
29. Quoted in Nancy Tomes, *The Gospel of Germs: Men, Women, and the Microbe in American Life.* Cambridge: Harvard University Press, 1998, p. 31.
30. Ott, *Fevered Lives*, p. 66.
31. Quoted in Rothman, *Living in the Shadow of Death*, p. 179.
32. Dubos, *The White Plague*, p. 104.
33. Quoted in Caldwell, *The Last Crusade*, p. 160.
34. Caldwell, *The Last Crusade*, p. 162.
35. Quoted in Tomes, *The Gospel of Germs*, p. 94.
36. Quoted in Dormandy, *The White Death*, p. 135.
37. Caldwell, *The Last Crusade*, p. 161.
38. Quoted in Caldwell, *The Last Crusade*, pp. 161–62.
39. Quoted in Ott, *Fevered Lives*, p. 64.

Chapter 3: The Bacillus's Deadly Work

40. Quoted in Rothman, *Living in the Shadow of Death*, p. 180.

41. Quoted in *Time International*, "TB: A Killer's Return," August 14, 2000, p. 22.

42. Jim Steele, interview with the author in Rockford, Illinois, June 16, 2001.

43. Dormandy, *The White Death*, p. 212.

44. Stephen Hall, "The Return of Tuberculosis—in a New, More Menacing Form," in *The Race Against Lethal Microbes: A Report from the Howard Hughes Medical Institute*. Chevy Chase, MD: Howard Hughes Medical Institute, 1996, p. 11.

45. Hall, "The Return of Tuberculosis," p. 11.

46. Quoted in *Business Week*, "TB Roars Back," October 2, 2000, p. 153.

47. Frank Ryan, *The Forgotten Plague: How the Battle Against Tuberculosis Was Won—and Lost*, Boston: Little, Brown, 1992, p. 23.

48. Paul Farmer, "TB Superbugs: The Coming Plague on All Our Houses" *Natural History*, April 1999, p. 46.

49. Keats quoted in Dormandy, *The White Death*, p. 13.

50. Quoted in Dubos, *The White Plague*, p. 104.

51. Quoted in Dubos, *The White Plague*, pp. 104–105.

Chapter 4: Going on the Offensive

52. Quoted in Rothman, *Living in the Shadow of Death*, p. 183.

53. Tomes, *The Gospel of Germs*, p. 124.

54. Quoted in Tomes, *The Gospel of Germs*, p. 126.

55. Quoted in Tomes, *The Gospel of Germs*, p. 126.

56. Quoted in Caldwell, *The Last Crusade*, p. 34.

57. Quoted in Chowder, "How TB Survived Its Own Death," p. 188.

58. Quoted in Tomes, *The Gospel of Germs*, p. 132.

59. Quoted in Rothman, *Living in the Shadow of Death*, p. 188.

60. Quoted in Rothman, *Living in the Shadow of Death*, p. 190.

61. Quoted in Rothman, *Living in the Shadow of Death*, p. 191.

62. Quoted in Dubos, *The White Plague*, p. 179.

63. Quoted in Dormandy, *The White Death*, p. 179.

64. Quoted in Dormandy, *The White Death*, p. 181.

65. Rothman, *Living in the Shadow of Death*, p. 159.

66. Quoted in Caldwell, *The Last Crusade*, p. 84.

67. Quoted in Caldwell, *The Last Crusade*, p. 78.

68. Quoted in Caldwell, *The Last Crusade,* p. 81–82.

69. Quoted in Caldwell, *The Last Crusade,* p. 38.

70. Chowder, "How TB Survived Its Own Death," pp. 185–86.

71. Chowder, "How TB Survived Its Own Death," p. 186.

72. Quoted in Chowder, "How TB Survived Its Own Death," pp. 190–91.

Chapter 5: Winning and Losing

73. Quoted in Dormandy, *The White Death*, p. 364.

74. Quoted in Rothman, *Living in the Shadow of Death*, p. 248.

75. Ryan, *The Forgotten Plague*, p. 385.

76. Quoted in Chowder, "How TB Survived Its Own Death," p. 192.

77. Quoted in Ryan, *The Forgotten Plague*, p. 399.

78. Quoted in Ryan, *The Forgotten Plague*, p. 393.

79. Quoted in Roberts, "The Comeback Plague," p. 50.

80. Quoted in Philip Hilts, "Rise of TB Linked to a U.S. Failure," *New York Times*, October 7, 1992, p. B4.

81. Jim Steele, interview with the author.

82. Quoted in Ryan, *The Forgotten Plague*, p. 399.

83. Ryan, *The Forgotten Plague*, p. 401.

84. Therese Cozzi, interview with the author in Edina, Minnesota, July 1, 2001.

85. Chowder, "How TB Survived Its Own Death," p. 94.

86. Therese Cozzi, interview with the author.

87. Quoted in Hall, "The Return of Tuberculosis," p. 11.

88. Farmer, "TB Superbugs," p. 46.

Chapter 6: Not Only a Medical Problem

89. Hall, "The Return of Tuberculosis," p. 20.

90. Quoted in Hall, "The Return of Tuberculosis," pp. 19–20.

91. Hall, "The Return of Tuberculosis," p. 20.

92. Quoted in Maura Lerner, "Tuberculosis Cases Rise in Minnesota," *Star Tribune*, March 23, 2001, p. B3.

93. Quoted in Roberts, "The Comeback Plague," p. 50.

94. Quoted in Yana Dlugy, "The Prisoners' Plague," *Newsweek International*, July 5, 1999, p. 18.
95. Dlugy, "The Prisoners' Plague," p. 18.
96. Kris Johnson, interview with the author in St. Paul, Minnesota, June 30, 2001.
97. World Health Organization, "Price of Vital TB Drugs Reduced by as Much as 94% Through WHO Partnership," July 19, 2001. www.who.int/inf-pr2001/en/pr2001-35.html.
98. Quoted in Dlugy, "The Prisoners' Plague," p. 18.
99. Quoted in Paul Farmer, *Infections and Inequalities: The Modern Plagues*. Berkeley: University of California Press, 1999, pp. 47–48.

FOR FURTHER READING

Books

David Ellison, *Healing Tuberculosis in the Woods: Medicine and Science at the End of the Nineteenth Century.* Westport, CT: Greenwood, 1994. Fascinating story of Edward Trudeau and his battle with tuberculosis.

Brent Hoff and Carter Smith III, *Mapping Epidemics: A Historical Atlas of Disease.* New York: Franklin Watts, 2000. Good summary of TB's history, treatment, and symptoms.

Katherine McCuaig, *The Weariness, the Fever, and the Feet.* Montreal: McGill-Queen's University Press, 1999. Somewhat difficult reading, but a good history of tuberculosis in Canada and how that nation has dealt with the disease both politically and socially. Helpful index.

Fred Ramen, *Tuberculosis.* New York: Rosen, 2001. Although information on the current state of tuberculosis research is limited, this book has a number of interesting sidebars, such as that of author George Orwell, who developed one of the earliest cases of drug-resistant TB.

Periodicals

Geraldine Baum, "An Ill Wind in New York Has Returned to Haunt a City Grappling with Poverty, AIDS, and a Fragile Health Care System," *Los Angeles Times*, November 10, 1991.

Business Week, "TB Roars Back," October 2, 2000.

Ken Chowder, "How TB Survived Its Own Death to Confront Us Again," *Smithsonian*, November 1992.

Current Events, "Comeback Killer," December 3, 1999.

Yana Dlugy, "The Prisoners' Plague," *Newsweek International*, July 5, 1999.

Paul Farmer, "TB Superbugs: The Coming Plague on All Our Houses," *Natural History*, April 1999.

Philip Hilts, "Rise of TB Linked to a U.S. Failure," *New York Times*, October 7, 1992.

Maura Lerner, "Tuberculosis Cases Rise in Minnesota," *Star Tribune*, March 23, 2001.

Pete Moore, "DOTS: What's in a Name?" *Lancet*, March 24, 2001.

Leslie Roberts, "The Comeback Plague," *U.S. News & World Report*, March 27, 2000.

Time, "TB—and Hope," March 3, 1952.

Time International, "The Death of a Nation: Drug Abuse, HIV and Tuberculosis, Combined with the Old Scourge of Alcoholism, Are Lowering Russia's Population," January 22, 2001.

Time International, "TB: A Killer's Return," August 14, 2000.

USA Today Magazine, "TB Easier to Transmit than Standard Test Reveals," February 2000.

WORKS CONSULTED

Books

Mark Caldwell, *The Last Crusade: The War on Consumption, 1862–1954*. New York: Atheneum, 1988. Excellent information on daily life in an American sanatorium.

Thomas Dormandy, *The White Death: A History of Tuberculosis*. New York: New York University Press, 1999. Excellent background on tuberculosis in ancient times. Fine bibliography.

René and Jean Dubos, *The White Plague: Tuberculosis, Man, and Society*. 1952. Reprint, New Brunswick, NJ: Rutgers University Press, 1987. René Dubos was a microbiologist who did much important TB work in the mid-twentieth century; his wife, Jean, experienced the disease firsthand. Well written and good background on early research.

Paul Farmer, *Infections and Inequalities: The Modern Plagues*. Berkeley: University of California Press, 1999. Challenging reading in some parts, but extremely well documented, with a great deal of current information about the politics of TB.

Stephen Hall, "The Return of Tuberculosis—in a New, More Menacing Form," in *The Race Against Lethal Microbes: A Report from the Howard Hughes Medical Institute*. Chevy Chase, MD: Howard Hughes Medical Institute, 1996. Excellent photography of TB bacillus and genetic technologies.

John Bessner Huber, *Consumption: Its Relation to Man and His Civilization, Its Prevention and Cure.* Philadelphia: J. B. Lippincott, 1906. Fascinating because of the era in which this was written. Good photographs and interesting section on government-run hospitals.

Katherine Ott, *Fevered Lives: Tuberculosis in American Culture Since 1870.* Cambridge: Harvard University Press, 1996. Good gathering of illustrations and photographs, as well as an interesting detailing of sanatoriums in the United States.

Sheila Rothman, *Living in the Shadow of Death: Tuberculosis and the Social Experience of Illness in American History.* New York: Basic Books, 1994. Well researched, with excellent notes.

Frank Ryan, *The Forgotten Plague: How the Battle Against Tuberculosis Was Won—and Lost.* Boston: Little, Brown, 1992. Interesting details of the infighting and competitiveness of researchers. Helpful notes.

Nancy Tomes, *The Gospel of Germs: Men, Women, and the Microbe in American Life.* Cambridge: Harvard University Press, 1998. Good notes and a fascinating photograph section.

Edward Livingston Trudeau, *An Autobiography.* Garden City, NY: Doubleday Page, 1916. Extremely readable account of Trudeau's early life, his bouts with TB, and his experiments with cures.

Internet Sources

World Health Organization, "Price of Vital TB Drugs Reduced by as Much as 94% Through WHO Partnership," July 19, 2001. www.who.int/inf-pr2001/en/pr2001-35.html.

INDEX

PICTURE CREDITS

ABOUT THE AUTHOR

Gail B. Stewart received her undergraduate degree from Gustavus Adolphus College in St. Peter, Minnesota. She did her graduate work in English, linguistics, and curriculum study at the College of St. Thomas and the University of Minnesota. She taught English and reading for more than ten years.

She has written over ninety books for young people, including a series for Lucent Books called The Other America. She has written many books on historical topics such as World War I and the Warsaw ghetto.

Stewart and her husband live in Minneapolis with their three sons, Ted, Elliot, and Flynn; two dogs; and a cat. When she is not writing she enjoys reading, walking, and watching her sons play soccer.